CULTS

CULTS

A BLOODSTAINED HISTORY

NATACHA TORMEY

FONTHILL

Fonthill Media Limited
Fonthill Media LLC
www.fonthillmedia.com
office@fonthillmedia.com

First published in the United Kingdom
and the United States of America 2014

British Library Cataloguing in Publication Data:
A catalogue record for this book is available from the British Library

ISBN 978-1-78155-279-7

The right of Natacha Tormey to be identified as the author of this work
has been asserted by him in accordance with the Copyright, Designs and
Patents Act 1988.

Typeset in 10pt on 13pt Sabon ST Ltd
Printed and bound by CPI Group (UK) Ltd, Croydon, CR0 4YY

Contents

Prologue 7

1 The Canaanite Genocide: Joshua 9

2 Zealots of Judea: The Siege of Masada 19

3 Islamic Crusade: Khalid ibn al-Walid 26

4 The Spanish Inquisition: Isabella, Ferdinand and Torquemada 36

5 Thugs: Killers and Thieves 46

6 The Family: Charles Manson 54

7 The People's Temple: Jim Jones 66

8 The Witch Doctor: Adolfo Constanzo 78

9 Prophet of Death: Jeffrey Lundgren 87

10 The Branch Davidians: David Koresh 95

11 Aum Shinrikyo: Shoko Asahara 108

12 Order of the Solar Temple: Joseph Di Mambro and Luc Jouret 124

13 Heaven's Gate: Marshall Applewhite 135

14 Movement for the Restoration of the Ten Commandments of God:
Joseph Kibweteere and Credonia Mwerinde 145

15 The Children of God: Ricky Rodriguez 154

Epilogue 169

Prologue

Throughout history, there is one thing that has consistently influenced the way that people live and how they interact—Religion.

Although religion has been a source of peace and prosperity, it has also been the cause of war, murder and destruction. In more recent history, religious groups that do not conform to the primary religions are often labelled cults. But what differentiates these cults from other faiths that have existed for hundreds or even thousands of years? When does an innocent belief turn into an excuse for torture, slaughter and racial or religious genocide? By looking back through history, we may assemble clues and note similarities that can help us to form an idea.

We begin our journey with Joshua's wars when he led the Hebrews to their Promised Land, leaving a trail of carnage behind them. We continue through time to the Zealot conflicts in Israel, the Islamic Crusaders and the Spanish Inquisition, finally reaching the stories of cult murders and suicides in the last two centuries. Throughout our journey, we will attempt to find answers to the many questions that surround such incidents.

How can an ordinary person or group of people be manipulated to such an extent that they willingly commit murder or take their own life? What drives the leaders of such movements to turn their followers into war machines or killers? Is religion in itself to blame, or are the culprits the interpreters of religious doctrines? Will society ever reach a point where religion is a personal belief, or will it always remain a tool that is used to gain wealth and power? And, lastly, when will it end?

I grew up in a cult, The Children of God, now known as The Family International. My experience makes it easier for me to recognise a cult and, as part of my journey into a normal life I looked back through history to identify the origins of cults. I found that they began almost as far back as historical records go. From the biblical times to modern day, they have not changed much apart from perfecting the skill of blending into society and hiding their true colours. Where will they be hiding next? What type of cover will they choose?

By looking at their prominent, common traits, we can educate the public as to how they can avoid being drawn into such 'families', 'support groups', 'causes' or whatever cover they use as a mask to hide what they truly are: a cult – an organised and obsessive form of religion that so often leads to tragedy and death.

Note from the author: Whilst I have strived to provide accurate information in this book, there may be inadvertent factual errors due to conflicting information that exists for certain subjects and events. Where I was faced with contradicting information, I have based my decision on what I believed to be the most reliable source.

CHAPTER 1

The Canaanite Genocide: Joshua

The story of Moses is legendary. The son of Jewish slaves, he was raised a prince among the Egyptian royal family but later defied the Pharaoh and went on to free the Hebrews from slavery. He led them on their journey towards the Promised Land; a sacred land that their God had guaranteed was their home, where they could worship him in peace and prosper.

I grew up with the stories of Moses and the Hebrew escape. During my childhood in a Christian cult, we were constantly fed biblical stories as part of our conditioning to ultimately become warriors in God's army. Their victories during their quest to conquer the Promised Land were key stories used to relate to us the importance of following God's calling and trusting him to lead us to victory. Following my departure from the cult at eighteen years of age, I revisited many of these biblical stories I had been brainwashed into believing were factual accounts. I wanted to form my own opinion about these characters. Were they really men of God, or was the biblical version a carefully edited account of historic events, twisted to support religious ideas?

What I discovered was a far cry from the heroic tales I had been told. The trail of blood that this quest for the Promised Land left behind is little known, but the truth is readily available in the chapters of the Bible that cover this period.

Hebrew-born Moses was raised in the royal court of Egypt after the Pharaoh's daughter, Princess Bithiah, rescued him from the river Nile when he was just a baby. The Pharaoh, feeling threatened by the growing number of Hebrew slaves, had done the unthinkable by ordering all Jewish children of the male gender be put to death. Moses' mother, in a desperate bid to save her son, placed him in a watertight basket, which she sent floating down the river Nile in the hope that someone would find him and keep him safe. When Princess Bithiah found him, she took him in, telling the royal court that he was her child. As such, he was raised as royalty, surrounded by wealth and given a fine education. But more importantly, he was passed on military training and strategic skills by none other than the Pharaoh himself. The powerful Egyptian ruler had no reason to suspect that the man he was training was not only a Hebrew, but also the very person who would later use these very skills to remove the Hebrew slaves from his empire.

The rest of the story is legendary. Moses fled Egypt after murdering an Egyptian who was beating a slave. He was taken in by a Midianite tribe which he married into and, during his time working as their shepherd, he received a message from God, commanding him to return to Egypt to free the Hebrews from slavery and lead them to the Promised Land. After a lengthy showdown with the Pharaoh they were finally allowed to leave, but the Egyptian ruler soon changed his mind and sent his army after the slaves. According to the Bible, the Red Sea miraculously parted and the Hebrew tribes were able to make an escape into the desert.

The story ends here for many people, but the truth is that the Hebrews' escape from Egypt was only the beginning of a long journey. And, as they travelled for many years across the desert, one man would increasingly stand out as Moses faded into old age. He was his closest assistant, the man to whom he would pass on his military knowledge and who would become his successor: Hoshe'a, better known as Joshua. The exact dates of his existence are not clear, but historians place his life between 1500–1390 BC.

Surprisingly, Joshua is not mentioned at all in the chapters of the Bible that cover the exodus from Egypt. It does, however, introduce him as Moses's right-hand man shortly after they left Egypt; on that basis, therefore, it would be reasonable to suggest that he must have been heavily involved in the organisation of this mass exit.

After the Hebrews left Egypt, they became vagabonds. A trail of tens of thousands of people snaked slowly through the dusty wilderness as they wandered, searching for the land that was promised to them. But, if they thought their journey would be a smooth and uneventful one, they were sorely mistaken. Not long after they set off into the scorching Sinai desert they were attacked by a fierce army of Canaanite warriors, the Amalekites, who began picking off the weaker members of the group who trailed behind the main core of the caravan.

Moses knew that they had to act; he turned to Joshua and asked him to lead their men into battle. It was a daunting prospect. They had limited armoury and their men were not warriors. Most would have been weak or already injured from years of hard labour as Egyptian slaves and, even those who were young and fit, were not professionally trained soldiers and had never fought together before. The outcome of the battle was incredibly uncertain but, with Egypt behind them, there was no option to turn back. They were trapped and left with no choice but to continue to move forward. In order to do that, they had to fight the Amalekites. It was a bloody battle and the amateur Hebrew army lost a great number of men; incredibly, however, they defeated them. This was Joshua's first military victory.

This battle gave Moses and Joshua even more power and together they maintained full control over their followers, regularly sentencing to death those who dared to rebel against their leadership. One demonstration of such harsh punishment occurred when Moses returned from his notorious journey to the top of Mount Sinai where he received the Ten Commandments. He had chosen his faithful assistant Joshua to accompany him part of the way and, on his return, they travelled back down together.

When they reached the rocky base of the mountain they were appalled to find that their people had been worshipping foreign idols in their absence, in particular a golden calf that represented an Egyptian deity. Furious, Moses ordered the death of 3,000 Hebrews as a statement to the others.

By making such a drastic decision, he and Joshua demonstrated key cult leadership behaviour. They chose to maintain control of their followers through fear. If we remove the legendary stories and look closer at the historical facts, it is clear that this is one of the first instances in history where we see the 'cult factor'. From hero to dictator, Moses swiftly became the feared leader of the people he fought so hard to deliver from slavery.

The former prince moved on to the next task at hand. He knew that, in order to make progress in their bid to conquer the Promised Land, he would need to raise a larger and more efficient army. And he knew just the man to lead it.

He sent Joshua with a team of elite soldiers on a reconnaissance mission. They were to assess the land to ensure it was prosperous and fertile; but, more importantly, they were to report back on what tribes lived on the land, their strength, their numbers and their military capacities.

Joshua and another spy, Caleb, brought back glowing reports on the prosperity of the land, carrying fruit, honey and milk back with them as proof. But they also brought back detailed descriptions of the fortified cities they had crossed on their journey. They had mapped thirty-one that were located on the land that they believed was rightfully theirs; these were populated by Canaanite tribes and communities that had lived on these territories for many years. As far as Joshua was concerned, these were cities that had to be destroyed and people that had to die.

But, according to the Bible, their quest towards the Promised Land was placed on hold at this stage as the Hebrews had continued to commit various sins such as idol worshipping, complaining about lack of food and doubting God and their leaders. Because of this, Moses told his people that God would not allow them into the Promised Land for forty years; that, instead, they would wander the barren desert as a punishment. Is this unlikely version of events really the truth, or were Joshua and Moses simply buying time? The older generation of the Hebrews that left Egypt were predominantly slaves who had been heavily influenced by Egyptian culture and beliefs. By now, many would have been worn down, aged and were most likely prone to discontent and rebellion against their oppressive leaders. Particularly if you consider that, despite their status as slaves, their lifestyle would not have been all that bad in Egypt. They would have had food to eat and roofs over their heads, albeit of poor standard for most. But now, here they were, wandering the scorching desert with barely enough food to stay alive and with only meagre tents and wild bushes as shade against the elements.

The new generation, which had been expanding since they had left Egypt, would have been entirely different. They were pure minded children that were being raised to have no other purpose than to participate in this quest for a new life. As such, they were their strongest asset and forty years would allow Moses and Joshua enough time to not only fabricate an arsenal of weapons, but also to allow this second generation to raise a brood of perfect soldiers, ones who were familiar with the terrain, having been trained in the vast wilderness from a young age. But, more importantly, they would be soldiers who were conditioned from birth to blindly serve the cause and follow Joshua into upcoming battles.

Sharing the land was not an option; Moses had informed his people that God would have it all or nothing at all. According to the Hebrews, the Canaanites worshiped idols, carried out human sacrifices and indulged in perverse sexual practices so they were not acceptable as neighbours. Either they had to leave of their own accord, or they were to be destroyed in a mission to cleanse the land and eliminate any risk of corruption, as described in the book of Deuteronomy 20:16-18:

> But of the cities of these people, which the Lord thy God doth give thee for an inheritance, thou shalt save alive nothing that breatheth. But thou shalt utterly destroy them; namely the Hittites, and the Amorites, the Canaanites, and the Perizzites, the Hivites, and the Jebusites; as the Lord thy God hath commanded thee. That they teach you not to do after all their abominations, which they have done unto their gods; so should ye sin against the Lord your God.

We see another clear cult factor here: isolation from outside influences. They did not trust their own people to live in close proximity to other cultures or religions out of fear that they would be polluted or influenced by them. Within a cult, isolation and separation from all possible temptation is crucial. It removes freedom of choice and allows the victim only one option, namely the cult leader's agenda.

Moses and Joshua regularly reminded their followers that this rule would have to be obeyed. Towards the end of the forty years, a deadly plague spread across the Hebrew settlement and people were dying in high numbers. Around the same time, Moses learnt that several of the Hebrew men were fornicating with neighbouring Moabite whores and he concluded that the plague was a punishment for this sin. He immediately pinned the blame on a Midianite tribe of nomads who lived amongst the Moabites, and instructed that they all be put to death.

It seems nonsensical for Moses to have decided to slaughter the very tribe that had taken him in years earlier when he fled Egypt. Especially as his own wife, Zipporah, was herself a Midianite, daughter of the tribe leader who had rescued him from the desert. Phineous, one of Moses' generals, is ordered to lead the assault. Joshua is not mentioned in this incident; by now, he was Moses' right-hand man and, as such, it is hard to imagine he would have had no involvement in the decision making prior to the assault.

Phineous and the Hebrew army attacked the Midianites, slaying every man as they had been instructed to do. But when it came to the women and children, the general could not bring himself to follow the order. In a brave move, he made the decision to take them as prisoners instead and he began to march them towards the Hebrew settlement.

Moses was furious when he learnt that Phineous had not followed his instructions and he sent soldiers to stop them before they arrived at the settlement. With the soldiers he sent a final order to Phineous—he was to immediately execute all the male children and the women who were not virgins. The general had no choice but to follow the command. The virgins were enslaved and approximately 60,000 women and male children were slaughtered that day.

The men who had to carry out the killings were ordered to stay outside the settlement for seven days in order to cleanse themselves. It is interesting that there is no mention of this type of cleansing period in any subsequent battle that the Hebrews fought in this campaign. I suspect that, as this was the first massacre they committed, the soldiers must have been somewhat traumatised and were perhaps being given time to compose themselves and come to terms with the atrocious murders they had been forced to commit. Little did they know that this was just the first of many massacres they would be instructed to carry out.

At the end of the forty years, they were finally ready to embark on their quest to conquer the Promised Land. They travelled from their settlement at Kadesh Barnea into the valley of the Jordan River. They crossed through Moab and Edom without any incidents but, when they reached Ammonite territory, they were forced to stop. Moses sent a messenger to the Ammonite king, requesting permission to cross through his land, but the king refused. The Hebrews had no choice but to prepare for battle against this kingdom that stood between them and the land that God had assured them was theirs.

Moses appointed Joshua as commander and he led their troops, now strong and experienced, on to the dry and rocky battlefield. The sheer scale of violence was unlike any of their previous battles. All living creatures were slaughtered and none were spared. Men, women, children, the elderly and cattle were all exterminated. Joshua was sending out a message to the Canaan cities ahead— 'this is your fate if you get in our way'.

Moses died not long after this battle. He never made it to the Promised Land, but he appointed his right-hand man to continue the quest. Joshua wasted no time in doing so. Eager to prove to his followers that he was a capable leader, he implemented a strategy that would result in full Hebrew control over Canaan. Their first target was an almost invincible enemy—not because of its size, but because of the notorious strength of its walls. Jericho was a relatively small city; it was roughly eight acres of land in size with a population of about 2,500 people. But its walls were another matter entirely. Up until that point they had been impenetrable, a fact that was well known to all.

Jericho is thought to have been one of the oldest cities known in history. Its twenty-five feet high double walls were designed to keep invaders out. If its outer walls were breached there was an inner wall, just as tall and strong that would also have to be overcome. Some habitants of Jericho lived in between or within the walls, which demonstrates just how wide these structures really were.

Joshua rallied his troops and crossed the river Jordan, sending two spies ahead into Jericho. They were to assess the city and report back so that he could put an appropriate strategy in place. The spies entered the city and made their way toward the nearest brothel—which may seem an odd choice, but really was quite clever as that would be one place where, as men travelling alone, they could pass unnoticed and make discreet enquiries about their military defence plans.

There they met Rahab, a whore who invited them back to her home which was located in the walls of the city. Before long, she realised that they were spies and, in a bid to spare herself and her family, she cleverly decided to join forces with them. She knew that the entire population of Jericho was gripped with fear; there was no doubt in her mind that the Hebrews would attack and eventually conquer their city. It was only a question of how and when.

As night fell, rumours that Hebrew spies had breached the city began to circulate. Soldiers spread out and patrolled the streets, anxiously searching for them. After a tip off, they knocked on Rahab's door and asked where the strangers were. She told them they had been there but had left not long before, pointing out the direction that they had taken. The soldiers rushed off in pursuit and Rahab called the spies down from her roof, where she had hidden them. The grateful spies promised her that her household would be spared if she tied a scarlet cord to her window sill so that they would know not to destroy that area of the wall. They escaped the city in the early hours of the morning by climbing down a rope strung from Rahab's window.

When the spies returned to the Hebrew camp, they informed Joshua that the people of Jericho were fearful and vulnerable and he decided that it was the perfect time to launch an attack. He led his army to the city and surrounded their walls. The city of Jericho was no match to Joshua's 9,000 soldiers but, even so, he decided not to launch a direct attack. Instead, he ordered his men to march around the city once a day, for six days and then, on the seventh day, they were to march around the city seven times before simultaneously blowing their trumpets and shouting at the top of their lungs. They obeyed and, on the seventh day, as they let out an almighty shout, the walls came crashing down. The Bible portrays the victory at Jericho as a miraculous event, but many historians believe that there is a practical explanation.

If the spies could escape from Rahab's window, then they could send soldiers in the same way. Was Rahab's red cord really a marker to let the Hebrews know which window was the one that would be their gateway into the city? Six days would have allowed ample time for Joshua to send in dozens of men, while the people of Jericho were being kept distracted by their unusual marching ritual around the walls.

Whatever the truth is, the outcome was inevitable. Apart from Rahab and her family, every living being was put to death and the city was burnt to the ground. Along with the total annihilation of all humans and animals, Joshua also gave strict instructions that nothing was to be taken from the cities they attacked; all of the silver, gold and bronze that they pillaged was to be placed into their holy treasury and all other items in the city were to be destroyed.

There would be no rest for the soldiers. Joshua was on a roll and his next target was Bethel, a city located in a strategic area of the mountainous region that controlled the trade routes for Canaan. Near Bethel were the ruins of the city of Ai. Joshua had no idea if the crumbling city was still occupied, but it was essential that he found out as he had to march his army past it, and he could not risk being attacked from the side as he made his way to wage war on Bethel. Knowing it was most likely empty, he sent an elite squad of 600 men to secure the site.

Unbeknown to him, although the city was abandoned, the Bethelite army had used the ruins to set up the perfect ambush. The trap worked and the Hebrew soldiers were slaughtered. Joshua was furious. This was his first military defeat; one that cast a shadow over his glorious victory at Jericho. He had to find someone to blame, and before long he found the perfect target.

He had recently learnt that one of his soldiers, Achan, had stolen gold, silver and a Babylonian garment from Jericho despite his strict instruction not to take anything. He told his followers that the ambush at Ai was God's punishment for the soldier's disobedience and, as a warning to the others, Joshua condemned Achan, his entire family and all of his animals to a public death by stoning.

Reassured that he had regained God's favour through the executions, Joshua led his men to the city of Ai. He headed into the ruins with just 1,000 men to lure the Bethelites out, leaving the remaining 8,000 out of sight behind nearby hills. His plan worked. The Bethelites, thinking they had the advantage, came out and met them.

The battle began and after only an hour, many of Joshua's men were killed and the few who were still alive began to flee. The Bethelites, thinking that they had won, went after the remaining men to finish them off. But they failed to notice a lone man at the top of a nearby hill. It was Joshua and he was sending signals to his hidden troops. Using his sickle sword against the sunlight, he flashed his command and a small unit snuck into the city and set it on fire.

The Bethelites walked straight into Joshua's genius trap. Behind them were the burning ruins and, before them, thousands of soldiers were closing in. They did not stand a chance. Their army was annihilated and their king was slaughtered and hung from a tree just outside the gates of his city. The city of Bethel surrendered.

For some reason, Joshua did not order the death of the population of Bethel city, but that is most likely because he formed a deal with them as he did with some of the other tribes he crossed on his journey through Canaan. Although he won many battles, he also lost many men and he had to constantly replenish his numbers. It is said that he recruited the men of these tribes and smaller cities in exchange for sparing their lives. Soon, he had not only replenished, but increased his numbers to 12,000 men, who he led to Gibeon.

The city of Gibeon was terrified. Having heard of the Hebrews' recent victories, they were not prepared to take them on. Instead, they made a deal with Joshua; their army would fight with him if he did not attack them. Working together, they caused a great deal of disruption to the five most powerful Canaanite kings and their kingdoms. They in turn, fearing invasion, formed the Amorite coalition led by Adonizedek, King of Jerusalem. He called upon the Kings of Hebron, Jarmuth, Lachish and Eglon to form an alliance and launch an offensive to stop Joshua. They led their 15,000 soldiers to Gibeon and surrounded the city. When Joshua learnt of this, he rushed his army there to honour their alliance.

In the middle of the night, the Hebrew army reached the outskirts of Gibeon. Joshua's military mind kicked into gear and he drew up a strategy, using the natural elements around him. He set his army into position amongst the brambles of the dry plains that surrounded the Amorite coalition's camp. He knew that he had little time, the sun was rising and that would be his greatest weapon.

It was the battle that biblical accounts refer to as 'the day the sun stood still'; where legends tell us that God froze the sun in the sky, allowing the Hebrews to fight in daylight until the battle was over. But the truth would have been substantially more realistic. The sun, rather than standing still, played a major part in their battle against this coalition. With dawn rising behind them, there would have been a window of time in which their adversaries, camped in the plains below, would have been completely blinded by the intense glare of the low-rising sun.

At daybreak, they attacked the coalition army who were utterly disadvantaged visually and, as they had done many times before, slaughtered every single man, even chasing down those who were running away. The five kings who had united in war against Joshua were amongst those slain that day. They had them executed and hung from trees outside the city.

But their day was not over yet. Joshua cashed in on the high morale amongst his troops and marched them onwards to Makkedah, where they killed every soul and, in the weeks that followed, they exacted the same fate on the cities of Libnah, Lachish, Eglon and Debir. In each city, they carried out their familiar murder campaign, leaving not a single living human or animal behind, as described in the book of Joshua 10:40.

> So Joshua smote all the country of the hills, and of the south, and of the vale, and
> of the springs and all their kings: he left none remaining, but utterly destroyed all
> that breathed, as the Lord God of Israel commanded.

Joshua did not complete the conquest of Canaan, although he made enormous progress towards that goal. For unknown reasons, he faded into anonymity in his old age and was buried alone in a place that, in Hebrew, translates as 'the angry mountain'. According to the Bible, he died at the age of 110 after twenty-eight years as the leader of the Hebrews, most of which were filled with carnage, mass murder and bloodshed.

There is one thing that struck me as I researched this epic event in history and the role that Joshua played in it. Despite obsessively following most of the rules that God had given them, Joshua, Moses and their people had completely ignored one of the Ten Commandments that God had given them on Mount Sinai. It is clearly defined in the book of Exodus 13:20.

Thou shalt not kill.

The instruction was clear and yet, in the name of their God, they did the contrary, claiming that the almighty had exceptionally allowed this genocide in order to cleanse the land that they were promised. They were not satisfied with killing just enemy soldiers in battle, they went beyond that by slaughtering innocent women, children and every living creature that they had labelled as corrupt.

In the book of Exodus, God gave Moses a number of instructions which, along with the Ten Commandments, were to form their book of laws. As a new nation, it was essential to set these guidelines as early as possible to maintain order within the twelve tribes of Israel. But, yet again, there is one rule in the twenty-third chapter that they completely disregarded.

Thou shalt not oppress a stranger for ye know the heart of a stranger, seeing as ye were strangers in the land of Egypt.

Oppression is too mild a word to describe the fate of their victims. It is tragic that the Hebrews forgot about their own suffering in Egypt and went on to inflict such horrors upon those who occupied Canaan.

To some, Joshua is still considered a hero and the Hebrews' victories in Canaan are still widely celebrated. But should they be? Should we ignore the reality of what occurred in favour of the legend?

CHAPTER 2

Zealots Of Judea:
The Siege Of Masada

It was AD 66 and the political situation in Israel was reaching breaking point. It had been over 1,300 years since Joshua had led the Hebrews to their Promised Land, but much had changed since. Wars had swept through their territory and they had been invaded by foreign empires such as the oppressive Seleucid Empire and the Roman Empire, who were currently in control.

Clusters of fanatical Jewish rebels known as zealots were not prepared to live peacefully under Roman rule and caused friction whenever they had the chance. After years of small-scale revolts, the rebellion had spread countrywide and the Romans were struggling to control these gangs of violent religious fanatics who valued independence over their own lives.

For the zealots, foreign rule was not an option; particularly when the foreigners were, in their eyes, idolaters whose presence would pollute their sacred land and turn their people away from God. The truth of the matter was that, in the majority of instances, the Romans never sought to prevent the Jews from practising their religion as long as they submitted to their occupancy and did not stir up trouble. They even allowed them to nominate their own king and High Priest for a number of years and gave them the power to enforce Jewish law and sort out their own internal affairs, just as they did when they condemned Jesus of Nazareth (Jesus Christ) to crucifixion despite the Roman Prefect, Pontius Pilate, voicing his doubts over the Nazarene's guilt.

The Romans were certainly not innocent parties; at times, they enforced their rule through violence and made examples of rebels by publically putting them to death. However, for the most part, they allowed the Jews to live as they had when they were independent. Granted, the situation was far from ideal—after all, no nation would choose to be occupied it if could be free. But the majority of Jews lived peacefully under Roman rule, with long periods of little or no disruptions.

But this was not one of them. The Romans were not known for their patience and, when the zealots refused to back down, they promptly brought in legions of military reinforcements to assist in a guerrilla war against the rebels, which continued over the next four years.

In AD 70, the Roman general Titus re-conquered Jerusalem and destroyed their temple, sending a clear message to the zealots that their rebellion was coming to an end. As their numbers dwindled, many of the remaining rebels trekked across the Judean wilderness and gathered at the fortress of Masada, a city built at the top of a high plateau that was said to be almost impregnable.

Built by King Herod the Great a century earlier, this incredible city in the southern district of Israel was built to act as a stronghold for the paranoid ruler who lived in fear that his people would one day revolt and overthrow him. Playing the role of a puppet Jewish king under Roman rule was a delicate position to manage, particularly when the zealots were always at hand to stir up violence and discontent. Not only did he have to constantly prove to the Romans that he could maintain control and the regular flow of tax payments, but he also had the difficult task of keeping his nation subdued and content despite the aforementioned taxes, which were constantly increasing and crippling the income of the commoners who made up the majority of his population.

But there was another threat that he feared even more and that was none other than Cleopatra, Queen of Egypt, who had openly expressed her interest in having Judea under her rule. With rumours circulating that Mark Antony was under Cleopatra's spell, Herod had good cause for concern. In a moment of carnal bliss, Mark Antony could hand Judea over to her and dethrone him as King. He needed a place of safety where he could lock himself away, should the political tide turn against him.

He built the fort with the intent that it would be completely self-sufficient and able to function for a long period under siege. The city had an impeccable view of the surrounding area, including Jordan and the Red Sea. Its walls were high and speckled with defence towers; there were large warehouses to store food and cisterns dug into the rock to collect rain water. Military barracks were built within the city along with more luxurious facilities, such as a three-tiered palace for the king, a swimming pool and bath houses. There was only one way to reach the city which was by trekking up a winding path that was so narrow that groups of people would have to travel in single file to make it to the top. This made it nearly impossible for any army to successfully move their troops, or any battle equipment, up to the city.

Over the next two years, a splinter group of extremist zealots called the Sicarii used the fortress as a base from which they would carry out regular assaults. Led by Eleazar ben Yair, the Sicarii were more fanatical than any other zealot group and were named after the *sicae*, a small dagger that they carried beneath their cloaks and which they would regularly use in attacks against the Romans, or even their own kind. Unlike most zealot groups, they often targeted other Jews, especially if they felt that they were in any way complying with Roman law or accepting foreign dominance. In one particular incident, they raided Ein-gedi, a village near Masada. Spurred by their fanatical faith, they surprised them in the middle of the night and slaughtered all those who were unable to run away. They took the lives of over 700 Jews and their only gain was the food supplies they stole from them.

Determined to put an end to the rebellion once and for all, the Roman governor Lucius Flavius Silva marched to Masada with the Tenth Legion in AD 72. When he reached the city, he surrounded the base of the mountain and his men set up camp, aware that they were most likely in for a long wait. Their biggest problem was the inaccessibility of the fort; to counter that issue, he commissioned an enormous ramp, which took over seven months to build. By using the landscape and moving thousands of tons of earth and rock, they constructed a ramp of over 300 feet in height and 600 feet in length, creating a long walkway that allowed his men to move a battering ram and other equipment to the base of the walls. With their war weapons now in position, they launched an assault of flying stones and fireballs at the wall and, before long, they were able to breach the fort. With the city now accessible, they made their final plans to invade.

Eleazar ben Yair knew that they were trapped. With the base of the mountain surrounded, there was no clear way for them to escape and, with the wall breached, it was simply a matter of time before the Romans invaded. He did not see surrender as an option. Refusing to be captured, he made one final speech to the habitants of the city. His speech was recorded by Josephus, a former Jewish military commander who had switched to the Roman side. He worked as their negotiator, but also kept very detailed historical records of the conflicts that were taking place around him:

However, neither did Eleazar once think of flying away, nor would he permit anyone else to do so; but when he saw their wall burned down by the fire, and could devise no other way of escaping, or room for their further courage, and setting before their eyes what the Romans would do to them, their children, and their wives, if they got them into their power, he consulted about having them all slain. Now as he judged this to be the best thing they could do in their present circumstances, he gathered the most courageous of his companions together, and encouraged them to take that course by a speech which he made to them in the manner following:

'Since we, long ago, my generous friends, resolved never to be servants to the Romans, nor to any other than to God himself, who alone is the true and just Lord of mankind, the time is now come that obliges us to make that resolution true in practice. And let us not at this time bring a reproach upon ourselves for self-contradiction, while we formerly would not undergo slavery, though it were then without danger, but must now, together with slavery, choose such punishments also as are intolerable; I mean this, upon the supposition that the Romans once reduce us under their power while we are alive. We were the very first that revolted from them, and we are the last that fight against them; and I cannot but esteem it as a favour that God hath granted us, that it is still in our power to die bravely, and in a state of freedom, which hath not been the case of others, who were conquered unexpectedly.

It is very plain that we shall be taken within a day's time; but it is still an eligible thing to die after a glorious manner, together with our dearest friends. This is what our enemies themselves cannot by any means hinder, although they be very desirous to take us alive. Nor can we propose to ourselves any more to fight them, and beat them. It had been proper indeed for us to have conjectured at the purpose of God much sooner, and at the very first, when we were so desirous of defending our liberty, and when we received such sore treatment from one another, and worse treatment from our enemies, and to have been sensible that the same God, who had of old taken the Jewish nation into his favour, had now condemned them to destruction; for had he either continued favourable, or been but in a lesser degree displeased with us, he had not overlooked the destruction of so many men, or delivered his most holy city to be burnt and demolished by our enemies.

To be sure we weakly hoped to have preserved ourselves, and ourselves alone, still in a state of freedom, as if we had been guilty of no sins ourselves against God, nor been partners with those of others; we also taught other men to preserve their liberty. Wherefore, consider how God hath convinced us that our hopes were in vain, by bringing such distress upon us in the desperate state we are now in, and which is beyond all our expectations; for the nature of this fortress which was in itself unconquerable, hath not proved a means of our deliverance; and even while we have still great abundance of food, and a great quantity of arms, and other necessaries more than we want, we are openly deprived by God himself of all hope of deliverance; for that fire which was driven upon our enemies did not of its own accord turn back upon the wall which we had built; this was the effect of God's anger against us for our manifold sins, which we have been guilty of in a most insolent and extravagant manner with regard to our own countrymen; the punishments of which let us not receive from the Romans, but from God himself, as executed by our own hands; for these will be more moderate than the other.

Let our wives die before they are abused, and our children before they have tasted of slavery; and after we have slain them, let us bestow that glorious benefit upon one another mutually, and preserve ourselves in freedom, as an excellent funeral monument for us. But first let us destroy our money and the fortress by fire; for I am well assured that this will be a great grief to the Romans, that they shall not be able to seize upon our bodies, and shall fall of our wealth also; and let us spare nothing but our provisions; for they will be a testimonial when we are dead that we were not subdued for want of necessaries, but that, according to our original resolution, we have preferred death before slavery.

Josephus goes on to describe the mixed reactions that Eleazar received after his speech with some zealots eager to carry out the mass suicide, but many others afraid and hesitant. Seeing their distress, he delivered another speech in which he dazzled his men by reminding them of the immortality of their souls and comparing death to a deep and peaceful sleep. In parts of his speech, he attempts to make them feel guilty for failing to comprehend that dying is their only option and then goes on to instil fear in their minds by describing the horrible acts of torture that the Romans would inflict on them.

This dramatic speech appears to persuade them all to jump on board with the plan. Josephus describes the way they went about the mass suicide in such clear detail that it is difficult not to visualise the horror of the scene when reading his words.

Now as Eleazar was proceeding on in this exhortation, they all cut him off short, and made haste to do the work, as full of an unconquerable ardor of mind, and moved with a demoniacal fury. So they went their ways, as one still endeavoring to be before another, and as thinking that this eagerness would be a demonstration of their courage and good conduct, if they could avoid appearing in the last class; so great was the zeal they were in to slay their wives and children, and themselves also! Nor indeed, when they came to the work itself, did their courage fail them, as one might imagine it would have done, but they then held fast the same resolution, without wavering, which they had upon the hearing of Eleazar's speech, while yet every one of them still retained the natural passion of love to themselves and their families, because the reasoning they went upon appeared to them to be very just, even with regard to those that were dearest to them; for the husbands tenderly embraced their wives, and took their children into their arms, and gave the longest parting kisses to them, with tears in their eyes. Yet at the same time did they complete what they had resolved on, as if they had been executed by the hands of strangers; and they had nothing else for their comfort but the necessity they were in of doing this execution, to avoid that prospect they had of the miseries they were to suffer from their enemies. Nor was there at length any one of these men found that scrupled to act their part in this terrible execution, but every one of them despatched his dearest relations. Miserable men indeed were they! whose distress forced them to slay their own wives and children with their own hands, as the lightest of those evils that were before them.

So they being not able to bear the grief they were under for what they had done any longer, and esteeming it an injury to those they had slain, to live even the shortest space of time after them, they presently laid all they had upon a heap, and set fire to it. They then chose ten men by lot out of them to slay all the rest; every one of whom laid himself down by his wife and children on the ground, and threw his arms about them, and they offered their necks to the stroke of those who by lot executed that melancholy office; and when these ten had, without fear, slain them all, they made the same rule for casting lots for themselves, that he whose lot it was should first kill the other nine, and after all should kill himself. Accordingly, all these had courage sufficient to be no way behind one another in doing or suffering; so, for a conclusion, the nine offered their necks to the executioner, and he who was the last of all took a view of all the other bodies, lest perchance some or other among so many that were slain should want his assistance to be quite despatched, and when he perceived that they were all slain, he set fire to the palace, and with the great force of his hand ran his sword entirely through himself, and fell down dead near to his own relations.

So these people died with this intention that they would not leave so much as one soul among them all alive to be subject to the Romans.

When the Romans reached the top of the ramp and entered the city the following day, they were met with a gruesome scene. Of the 967 habitants of the city, only two women and five children were still alive, having slipped away to hide in nearby caves. The remaining population of Masada was dead. The men had set fire to the fortress and killed their wives and children first. Then they drew lots and ten zealots were selected to put the others to death. When that was done, the final ten again drew lots and the man who lost killed the others before taking his own life. Corpses were strewn across the burnt remains of the city, leaving the Romans baffled as to just how far the zealots were willing to go to escape their rule.

Now for the Romans, they expected that they should be fought in the morning, when, accordingly, they put on their armor, and laid bridges of planks upon their ladders from their banks, to make an assault upon the fortress, which they did; but saw nobody as an enemy, but a terrible solitude on every side, with a fire within the place, as well as a perfect silence. So they were at a loss to guess at what had happened.

At length they made a shout, as if it had been at a blow given by the battering ram, to try whether they could bring any one out that was within; the women heard this noise, and came out of their under-ground cavern, and informed the Romans what had been done, as it was done; and the second of them clearly described all both what was said and what was done, and this manner of it; yet did they not easily give their attention to such a desperate undertaking, and did not believe it could be as they said; they also attempted to put the fire out, and quickly cutting themselves a way through it, they came within the palace, and so met with the multitude of the slain, but could take no pleasure in the fact, though it were done to their enemies. Nor could they do other than wonder at the courage of their resolution, and the immovable contempt of death which so great a number of them had shown, when they went through with such an action as that was.

In my opinion, there was nothing courageous or brave about the zealots' decision to commit mass suicide. They were able to fight when it came to slaughtering helpless men, women and children in the dark of night; but, when faced with the skilled soldiers of the Roman army, they saw no option but to kill their wives and children rather than fight to the end, even if it meant holding off the Romans long enough for some of their loved ones to attempt an escape. They did not appear to have even considered surrender. Nor did they try to negotiate with the Romans who, despite their reputation, could at times be surprisingly reasonable in battle.

According to the survivors who related the events of that night to Josephus, a substantial number of zealots were not on board with the mass suicide plan until Eleazar berated them with his second speech, which shows the psychological control that this zealot leader must have had over them. Like most cult leaders, he was bold and charismatic, which enabled him to spur those around him with religious fanaticism and make them believe that there was no other option but to commit the ultimate act of martyrdom.

As is so often the case, the children were the true victims of this tragedy. Unable to choose for themselves, their young lives were extinguished by a group of terrorists who used their religion as an excuse to steal, harass and kill.

CHAPTER 3

The Islamic Crusade:
Khalid Ibn Al-walid

Author's note: In this chapter, when I use the word 'crusade' it is in an Islamic context to represent a holy war or jihad.

'When I am in the battlefield I love it more than when I am in my house.'
Khalid ibn al-Walid

Born in Mecca *c*. AD 592, Khalid ibn al-Walid was one of the greatest warriors in Islamic history and a close companion of the prophet Muhammad.

His father, Walid ibn al-Mughira, was the chief of Banu Makhzum, one of the three leading tribes of the Arabic Quraysh clan. When Khalid was just an infant he was sent to a Bedouin tribe in the desert for a few years so that he could be raised in an unpolluted environment, as was common practice amongst Quraysh tribes. When he returned to his family in Mecca at around the age of six he began his training in warfare, which the Banu Makhzum tribe specialised in. As a young man he was a champion wrestler, an expert horse rider and well-trained in the use of war weapons, including spears, bows and swords.

Around them, conflict was brewing as Muhammad's new faith spread across the surrounding Arab territories. Khalid's father was known for his opposing stance against the new Islamic faith and, when the Muslims closed in on the Quraysh tribes, tensions climaxed resulting in the Battle of Badr. Muhammad himself was originally from a Quraysh tribe, the Banu Hashim, but had been forced to migrate to the nearby city of Medina, as the radical doctrines he was teaching did not go down well in his hometown. But Mecca, being one of the wealthiest cities in the area, was a key territory that Muhammad knew he would have to conquer in order to assert his authority and solidify his position as a religious leader.

When Khalid's brother, Walid ibn Walid, was taken prisoner during the battle, his father sent him and his elder brother to Medina to pay a ransom for his freedom. They were successful and Walid was released. However, on their way back to Mecca, their newly liberated brother fled and returned to his captors in Medina, where he converted to Islam.

Khalid was baffled but with no other course of action open to them, he and his elder brother returned to Mecca, where they strengthened their defences and prepared for the likely possibility that the Muslims would attack them again. They were right. The following year, in 625, Khalid played a key role in the Battle of Uhud when he took advantage of a breach in the Muslim battle line and led his cavalry into the heart of their army, causing chaos and confusion amongst their ranks. Khalid and his men slaughtered many Muslim soldiers and Muhammad was severely injured in the battle, leaving his men with no other option but to retreat into the ravines of Mount Uhud. Neither side won or lost the battle. It was inevitable, therefore, that another battle would have to be fought and just two years later, the scent of war filled the air again. In a bid to wipe out the Muslim army, comprising some 3,000 men, Arab and Jewish tribes formed a confederacy and set off towards the city of Medina. With an estimated 10,000 men and 600 horses, this battle should have been a quick win for the confederacy, but Muhammad cleverly used the natural fortifications of the city to his advantage. He ordered his men to dig a deep ditch between the city and the enemy, which would render their cavalry useless. The battle was at a standstill for over three weeks as Khalid and his men kept the city under siege, but had no clear route by which to launch an attack.

As the weeks progressed, there was friction between the allies of the confederacy. With a mutual lack of trust between the tribes, arguments were rife and accusations broke down communications. Their provisions were beginning to run low and their soldiers and horses were going hungry. To add to that, the climate took a turn for the worse; temperatures dropped and gale force winds ripped through their camp, snuffing out their fires and tearing down their tents. It left them exposed to the elements without adequate shelter or heat for days on end. After three weeks they could take no more and, one cold night, they retreated.

But Muhammad was not about to let them go that easily. In a show of strength, he led his men to the nearby Jewish Banu Qurayza settlement, where there was a tribe who had been part of the confederacy. They held the city at siege for twenty-five days until they surrendered and, when they did, he instructed his men to dig pits and behead all the men of the city. It is estimated that 400–900 men were beheaded that day; the women and children were taken as slaves.

Muhammad had now established himself as a religious and political leader and, so as to avoid death and destruction, a few of the tribes in the surrounding areas converted to Islam and a peace treaty was put into place between the Muslims and the Quraysh tribes of Mecca. Khalid's newly converted brother began sending him numerous letters urging him to convert. Eventually, in 629, he agreed and he travelled to Medina to meet the Islamic prophet and accept the Muslim faith.

Muhammad soon realised that Khalid had exceptional military skills and this, coupled with his fanatical passion for his new faith, made him extremely valuable. The young fighter embraced the belief that all nations of the world must submit to Allah and accept Sharia law; as a result, and with the prophet's encouragement, he decided to dedicate his life to making war against all those who refused to convert to Islam.

A few months after his arrival in Medina, he had his first opportunity to prove his loyalty when Muhammad sent him as fourth in command of his army to fight in the battle of Mutah against the Eastern Roman Byzantine Empire.

As before, the Muslim army was sorely outnumbered. With only 3,000 men, they stood no chance against the 200,000 men of the Roman and Arab allied army; incredibly, however, they were not deterred. Believing that martyrdom was an honourable death, they marched forward and engaged in battle.

All three Muslim commanders were killed, leaving Khalid solely in charge of a disastrous military defeat. In a tactical move, he managed to distract the enemy and retreat before his entire army was wiped out. It was reported that the fighting in this battle was so intense that Khalid used a total of nine swords, as the blades of the first eight snapped under the force of his blows. Hence, Muhammad bestowed upon him the name Sayf Allah al-Maslul, meaning 'the Sword of Allah'.

Soon after this battle, the ten-year treaty that had been previously agreed between the Muslims and the Quraysh tribes fell apart, which led to the conquest of Mecca. Muhammad divided his army into four columns, one of which he placed under Khalid's command, and they closed in on Mecca simultaneous from all four sides of the city, leaving its inhabitants no chance of escape. The city surrendered with no casualties, apart from those caused by Khalid and his men, who slaughtered twelve Meccan soldiers on their way into the city.

They were on a mission and would not cease until they had fulfilled their quest to conquer and convert all non-Muslim territories for as far as they could reach. One after another they attacked and invaded cities further and further afield. The Battle of Hunayn soon followed in 630, with seventy Hawazin enemy soldiers killed, whilst the others fled. Six thousand women and children were taken as slaves and their spoils were claimed by the Muslims, including 24,000 camels. Most of the Hawazin men fled to nearby Ta'if, which led to a siege of the city. The Muslim army surrounded the city for two weeks but were unable to penetrate and eventually retreated, with Muhammad leaving behind a promise that they would return and capture the city.

The distraught residents were terrified and sent a delegation to Mecca. They asked the prophet to allow them to worship their Goddess Al-lat for a further three years, but he refused, promising them that he would make good on his word and return to take control of the city. Eventually, the Ta'if inhabitants realised that they had no choice and they surrendered.

Khalif took part in all of these battles and gained a reputation as a fierce warrior. The Muslim army was growing each month and they now had 30,000 men, a far cry from their humble beginnings.

The Battle of Tabouk followed just a few months later—although, by most accounts, there was no battle at all. Muhammad had marched his army towards the city of Tabouk to fight the Byzantine army as he had learnt they were preparing an attack against him. However, when they arrived, there was no one there to fight. As it turned out, they had been fooled by a rumour that held no truth behind it. The journey, however, served as a successful political campaign. Many Arab tribes they crossed along the way, impressed by the size of their army and their recent victories, decided to break off their alliance with the Byzantine Empire and join the Muslims instead.

In 631, Khalid was sent on several missions by Muhammad, one of which was a journey to the Banu Jadhimah tribe to invite them to convert to the Islamic faith. Upon arrival, the tribe's members began to protest that they already had their own religion and Khalid, furious at their refusal and also spurred on by past grievances he'd had against this particular tribe, began to execute them one by one until he was stopped by one of this peers. When Muhammad heard of his actions, he was very angry and cried out over and over, 'O God, I am innocent of what Khalid has done!' The Islamic leader felt obliged to pay compensation to the families of Khalid's victims, yet he retained the bloodthirsty commander in his service.

Muhammad then sent him to invade the city of Dumatul Jandal and destroy their idol Wadd, which represented their God of love and friendship. The inhabitants of the city resisted and Khalid slaughtered the majority of them. Cities that did not comply faced the annihilation of their male population, with women and children taken captive to be held as prisoners or sold as slaves. Those that did comply were often forced to convert or, allegedly, were given the option to retain their religion if they paid *jizyah*, a very high tax that allowed non-Muslims to live on Muslim territory under Islamic military protection. For many cities, this tax was simply unaffordable and most eventually converted out of fear of continued attacks or death.

On this subject, Khalid made the following statement to those whom he conquered:

> I call you to God and to Islam. If you respond to the call, you are Muslims: You obtain the benefits they enjoy and take up the responsibilities they bear. If you refuse, then you must pay the jizyah. If you refuse the jizyah, I will bring against you tribes of people who are more eager for death than you are for life. We will fight you until God decides between us and you.

When Muhammad died in June 632, the Islamic crusade escalated under the leadership of Abu Bakr. It would appear that, with their prophet dead, the Muslim army was no longer restrained and they went forward in their quest with a level of barbaric violence that, no doubt, their deceased founder would not have approved of. Abu Bakr also put a stop to offering freshly conquered lands the option to pay jizyah, only leaving them the choice to convert or die.

Following Muhammad's death, many of the Arab tribes who had joined forces with him went on to turn against the Muslim army. Abu Bakr chose Khalid, now a military commander, as his advisor and they went on the offensive to hunt down the rebel tribes. They led their army to central Arabia, where they slaughtered men, women and children in the battles of Ghamra, Naqra and Zafar.

Khalid honed in on the Banu Tamim tribes, who all gave in without putting up a fight, apart from the Banu Yarbu tribe. Their leader, Sheikh Malik ibn Nuwayrah did not surrender but, in a demonstration of goodwill, tried to avoid a battle by paying a hefty amount of tax to the city of Medina. Khalid was not satisfied. He accused Malik of rebellion and tracked him down in the desert. He arrested him and had him executed along with his men. He then went on to cause controversy when he married Malik's widow, Layla.

One of his men, a close friend of the deceased Muhammad, was outraged and returned to Medina to report what he had seen to Abu Bakr. Rumours were already circulating that Khalid had killed Malik solely because he wanted to marry his wife, and the fact that Malik was a converted Muslim made this murder all the more serious. Abu Bakr called his commander back to base for questioning, but no further action was taken against him. After all, Khalid was far too valuable for their cause. His military knowledge and religious zeal could make all the difference in a battle and he was about to prove his worth once more when he went on to crush their most powerful enemy, Musaylimah, from the district of Yamaha, a self-proclaimed prophet who had been Muhammad's greatest rival when he was alive.

The battle of Yamaha took place in December 632. The two armies clashed in blood-soaked combat as each fought for their God and their religion. It is said that, in one gulley, there had been so much carnage that a stream of human blood flowed down the city streets into a ravine. Such was the violence that the two armies had to halt the fighting so that their men could rest before carrying on again.

Both sides suffered great casualties but, in the second half of the battle, the Muslims began to gain the advantage. As they were reaching the end of the fight, Musaylimah and the 7,000 men he had left retreated to a garden surrounded by high walls where they awaited Khalid and his assassins. When they arrived, the final episode of this battle was as gory as the rest of it. Every one of the 7,000 men in the garden was slaughtered, including Musaylimah, who was speared with a javelin and then beheaded. The garden was then named 'The Garden of Death' and the rebellion amongst the tribes came to an end.

With their lands now secure, Abu Bakr decided to start another campaign to expand their territory. He sent orders to Khalid, who was still in Yamaha, instructing him to invade the Sassanid Persian Empire province of Iraq. Khalid set out with 10,000 men, sending a message ahead of him to Hormuz, the Persian governor of Dast Meisan. As this empire was extremely wealthy, they were given the rare option to pay *jizyah*:

> Submit to Islam and be safe. Or agree to the payment of the Jizyah, and you and your people will be under our protection, else you will have only yourself to blame for the consequences, for I bring the men who desire death as ardently as you desire life.

Troops from Arab tribes joined them on the way and they entered Persia with an army of 18,000 men. The Sassanid army was approximately the same size and was primarily made up of Christian Arabs. They were, however, one of the strongest armies of that period in history. With powerful weaponry and heavy armour, they would be a difficult opponent to beat. But Khalid played this to his advantage. He tired out the Sassanid army by changing the position of his troops over and over again, forcing the heavily armoured soldiers to march back and forth in a bid to launch a head-on attack. Finally, when he knew they were exhausted, he prepared to face them in battle. The Sassanid army, once in formation, linked themselves with chains in a bid to demonstrate that they would rather die than lose the battle; the chains also made it harder for their enemy to breech their formation.

Just before the 'battle of chains' was due to commence, Hormuz challenged Khalid to a duel. It couldn't have worked out better for the Muslims as Khalid won the duel and they went on to launch a full-scale attack on the exhausted Sassanid army. They penetrated their formation and began slaughtering their troops. Most of the Sassanid men who were not chained were able to escape, but those who were had no choice but to await death and thousands were killed on that day in the name of Allah.

Next, Abu Bakr sent Khalid to the Eastern Roman Empire. Khalid and his men crossed the scorching Syrian desert and won a great victory at the battle of Ajnadayn, located in present day Israel. As with his previous battles, despite being sorely outnumbered, he went to extremes to exterminate his enemy. It is estimated that 50,000 Roman soldiers were massacred that day.

Damascus was next on his list. In 634, his army surrounded the city and held it at siege for thirty days. During the siege, Abu Bakr died but, soon after, they successfully entered the city and slaughtered thousands of its inhabitants.

With Bakr now dead, Umar, Khalid's cousin, was chosen to replace him. Umar immediately relieved Khalid of his position as commander of the Muslim army, despite his high profile and immense popularity. He told his advisors that he did not have anything against Khalid, but had only dismissed him to remind people that Allah was the one who gave victory, not a man. But the rumours told otherwise. Umar had been unimpressed with his cousin over the scandal surrounding his marriage to Malik's widow and, since, with Khalid's increasing power and popularity, their relationship had deteriorated. It is likely that Umah felt threatened by Khalid and was removing his main source of power before he had an opportunity to overthrow him.

Incredibly, Khalid refused to leave the army and instead accepted a demotion. He became a lower level commander reporting to Abu Ubaidah, the man who replaced him. Together, they headed straight into another fight at the battle of Fahl in Jordan, where they killed another 10,000 Roman soldiers. Following that victory, they went north into Syria where they held the city of Emesa at siege for a lengthy four months, until they finally broke into its walls in March 636 and massacred thousands of its habitants. Khalid's military knowledge and vicious battle skills did not go unnoticed by his commander, who began to heavily rely on him for advice.

With such frequent and intense battles ongoing between the Muslim army and the Byzantine Roman Empire, it was only a matter of time before the conflict reached its climax. And it did later that year in August, when they came head to head in the battle of Yarmouk. It was a decisive battle and one which both sides could not afford to lose. With 40,000 men on the Arab side and 100,000 men on the Roman's, it was destined to be a bloody and gruesome affair. The battle dragged on for six long days and resulted in a historic win for the Muslims. The Roman army lost over half its men and were crushed, resulting in the collapse of the Byzantine Empire in Syria.

With their crusade going strong, they travelled on to Jerusalem, which did not fall easily into their hands. It took four months of siege before they surrendered in April

637. From there, the Muslim invaders took over the remainder of northern Syria and attempted to conquer Armenia and Anatolia unsuccessfully, partly because Khalid was called back to Medina to face accusations that he had fraudulently dipped into money from the military treasury. Despite that, Khalid returned a hero, adored by the people for his victories and the expansion of their territory. Umar was more than ever under threat by him and he used this accusation to sideline Khalid once and for all, dismissing him from the army in 638. As he had done before, Umar issued a statement to his people to mask his hidden agenda:

> I have not dismissed Khalid because of my anger or because of any dishonesty on his part, but because people glorified him and were misled. I feared that people would rely on him. I want them to know that it is Allah who give us victory; and there should be no mischief in the land.

In 642, just four years after Khalid's dismissal, he died at home. It is said he was very unhappy that he was not able to fulfil his dream of dying as a martyr for Allah. On his deathbed, he expressed his discontent:

> I've fought in so many battles seeking martyrdom that there is no spot in my body left without a scar or a wound made by a spear or sword. And yet here I am, dying on my bed like an old camel. May the eyes of the cowards never rest.

The crusade did not end there and, by 655, they had expanded even further, breaching into European territory and slaughtering infidels on their way.

Khalid left behind a legacy as a hero of the Muslim faith, a strong warrior anointed by God. A mosque was dedicated to him in the Syrian city of Homs and his tomb was placed inside. It has become a pilgrimage site for Muslims to this day. But incredibly, as I was writing this chapter in July 2013, news broke that his tomb had been completely destroyed by army shelling in the ongoing conflict that is taking place in Syria.

But really, when we look past the glorious tales of Khalid's victories, we see a much darker story that unfortunately has plagued the past of most of the world's prominent religions. They killed for Allah. They were prepared to die as martyrs for their God rather than show tolerance by living side by side with other religions. They slaughtered hundreds of thousands of non-Muslim people just because they were not of the same religion. The Islamic conquest was in effect religious genocide. There was no need to kill so many people to expand their territory; it could have taken place with very little loss of life, but religion got in the way. They did not kill out of self-defence. They killed out of fanatical, religious self-righteousness and the arrogant belief that their God had commanded them to convert the entire world to Islam and kill any infidels who refused to accept their religion.

To this day, Muslim terrorists still hold on to this belief and, when they murder thousands of innocents, they are convinced that, like Khalid, they are carrying out holy *jihad* and ridding the world of infidels. If they die doing so, they believe that, as a martyr, they have fulfilled their highest calling.

Following the 9/11 attacks in the United States, it was reported Bin Laden often referred to westerners as crusaders, in reference to the deaths that the Christian crusaders caused during the notorious first and subsequent crusades. However, he omits to mention that the Muslim crusade took place long before the Christian crusade and, more importantly, that the Christian crusades actually began as a defensive war to hold off the Muslim army who were attempting to invade Europe. In 1094, Byzantine emperor Alexius Comenus I begged the western Christian nations for help to hold back the Muslim army from invading his territory following over 400 years of aggressive Islamic expansion. Over two thirds of the old Christian world had already been conquered by the Muslims; if they did not begin to push back, Europe would be next.

The following year, Pope Urban II preached the first crusade and called upon knights to defend the western European nations. But somehow it soon turned into a religious holy war, which resulted in torture and death being inflicted on their victims, just as the Muslims had been doing for centuries.

What the Christian crusade became was just as horrific as any religious murder spree, and sadly I do not believe that we have seen the end of such religious crimes. From the earliest points of history, it is clear that religion has been the cause of many conflicts and wars. This is not a new phenomenon and there are not many religions that can claim they have never used violence or caused death in the name of their religion.

If we are to agree with Bin Laden's theory, that the West deserved punishment for the pain they inflicted on Muslim nations, then just about every nation on earth should be at war with another nation who, at some point in distant history, may have invaded and pillaged their country.

On the subject of forced conversions, Muslim apologists claim that there were none, as the only way a conversion is forced is if it is obtained by hanging a sword above the victim's neck, essentially threatening to bring down the sword if they do not have a change of heart. And, since there is no evidence of any instance in which this particular scenario occurred during the Islamic expansion, they have concluded that there no forced conversions took place. It would appear they did not consider threat of attack, rape, slavery and death as matters to consider when reaching that conclusion.

There are passages in the *Qur'an* that clearly support such acts of violence.

Qur'an 8:65
O Prophet, urge the faithful to fight. If there are twenty among you with determination they will vanquish two hundred; if there are a hundred then they will slaughter a thousand unbelievers, for the infidels are a people devoid of understanding.

Qur'an 9:5
When the sacred forbidden months for fighting are past, fight and kill the disbelievers wherever you find them, take them captive, torture them, and lie in wait and ambush them using every stratagem of war.

Qur'an 47:4
So, when you clash with the unbelieving Infidels in battle, smite their necks until you overpower them, killing and wounding many of them. At length, when you have thoroughly subdued them, bind them firmly, making captives. Thereafter either generosity or ransom until the war lays down its burdens. Thus are you commanded by Allah to continue carrying out Jihad against the unbelieving infidels until they submit to Islam.

Islam, as with all religions, is predominantly made up of devoted followers who strive to live a sincere and peaceful life according to their religious beliefs and traditions. Many of their doctrines are positive and based on respect, kindness and clean living. Did Muhammad intend to create such a violent streak that runs through the Islamic religion, or were his words misinterpreted and taken out of context? We will never know; but, as with all religions, the good is so often overshadowed by the fanatics who commit heinous acts in the name of their God. Be it the Christian or Islamic crusades, both faiths were tarnished by the violence and oppression that certain individuals exerted on others simply because they believed that their religion was the only one that was right.

CHAPTER 4

The Spanish Inquisition: Isabella, Ferdinand and Torquemada

When I was researching various cults to write about in this book, I could not help but cross many references to prominent Christian churches, such as the Catholic or Protestant church. But, to classify them as a cult would be inaccurate, although many would claim they are the largest cults of them all. If that was the case, then all primary religions would be cults, including Islam, Judaism, Buddhism and Hinduism. It is a very interesting subject of debate. Where is the line between a religion and a cult? How far should a religion be allowed to go in terms of the power and wealth that they have?

However, if we break it down, we begin to realise they do not hold the key 'cult factors' that most cults do. Although each of the above-mentioned religions have and still do cause death and wars, in the majority of instances this is down to one or several people who use these religions as an excuse for the bloodshed of innocents. They are not cults, but fundamental religions from which cults have emerged—spin-off religions, so to speak. Almost every cult originates from one of these primary religious groups, but it is that twist, the interpretation of their religion and that fanatic behaviour, that turns them into a cult.

One such example is the Inquisition, which directly emerged from the Catholic Church.

Christianity grew rapidly following the death of Christ in approximately AD 33. But, as the Church grew, so did its need for leadership, organisation and rules. By the early twelfth century the loose management structure that was in place allowed heresy to creep its way into their ranks. From excessive drinking to gambling and fornication, even priests and nuns fell into the lure of materialism and greed.

In a bid to control their crumbling church, Catholic leaders set up the global papal structure that exists to this day. They set the laws of the Church and laid down religious practices that Christians should follow, slowly centralising their administration and solidifying their control over all Christian groups and their influence with royalty and governments. Heresy, which was once tolerated, became a legitimate excuse for righteous persecution.

Needless to say, the increasing power of the Church did not go unnoticed by some. By the early thirteenth century, groups of Christians across Europe began to resist the changes. In their opinion, the Church itself was veering away from its God-given role as spiritual leader and, instead, was seeking to gain material wealth and political power. These Christians began to break away from the controlling clutch of the Papacy and formed their own religious groups. Some were small fellowships led by former crusaders or missionaries, while others were more prolific, such as the Cathars and the Waldensians, who would later become dangerous heretics in the eyes of the Church.

With time, the word *heretic* took on a very different, darker meaning. Rather than being a word that was used to describe a Christian who had lost their path, it became a term for a Christian who had been corrupted and who was poisoning the sacred holiness of the Church. They were a danger to all true Christians and they had to be stamped out. As the Inquisition progressed, the definition of the term heretic widened to include just about any person who did not conform to the Catholic way of living.

The general term, the Inquisition, actually encompasses several separate inquisitions that took place over hundreds of years, including the medieval inquisition which began in 1184, the Roman inquisition in 1542, the Portuguese inquisition in 1536 and the Spanish inquisition. The latter is the most notorious of them all, predominantly because of the barbaric acts of torture that took place, but also due to the cruel nature of one inquisitor in particular, Torquemada. It is important to note that such acts of torture were carried out in all other inquisitions, notably the medieval inquisition, which is said to have had a higher record of torture and death than in Spain.

The Tribunal of the Holy Office of the Inquisition began in 1478. It was a movement created by the Spanish monarchs, Ferdinand II of Aragon and Isabella I of Castile, a fervent Catholic. They had been wed to unite Spain and, together, they decided that in order to bring about full unity in their realm, they would have to amalgamate their nation's religious beliefs. They decreed that Spain would officially become a Catholic realm.

Initially, the purpose of the Inquisition was to force habitants of foreign religions to convert to the Catholic Church and, more importantly, to sniff out the heretics and 'conversos' amongst their Catholic population. Conversos was the term given to people of non-Catholic religious beliefs, predominantly Jews, Muslim Moors and Protestants, who had converted to Catholicism to enhance their business opportunities or social standing but whom, behind closed doors, were still practising their own religion in secret.

This phenomenon had begun in 1391 when there was a spate of massacres against the Jews in Spain, forcing many to convert to Christianity to avoid the same fate. Although Catholic priests and the Spanish population doubted the sincerity of this sudden change of faith, they tolerated it for some time. However, since then, some of these conversos had married into the Spanish aristocracy or had thrived in business, becoming increasingly powerful and wealthy. The Spanish royal family and nobles felt that something had to be done to crush this conversos issue that threatened the very stability of Spain.

As the monarchs planned their next move, explosive clashes erupted between conversos and the Catholic Church; they knew they had to act quickly, before they had a nationwide uproar on their hands. King Ferdinand approached Pope Sixtus IV requesting a papal order to create an inquisition, which would allow him to enforce the Catholic religion across their country. In his petition, he asked that the Pope grant him permission to name his own inquisitors to carry out the task; a demand that would give him sole authority to purge the occupants of Spain under the cover of the Catholic Church's holy blessing.

Initially, the Pope refused and made an attempt to issue a papal bull to block the request as he knew that, by granting it, Ferdinand would have full power to act under the papacy's name. But Ferdinand held one very valuable card. He knew that Rome was under threat of attack by the Turks and that they could not afford to lose one of their strongest allies, Spain. By threatening to withhold military support, the Spanish king obtained the outcome he was looking for when the papal order was granted on 1 November 1478, giving him and his queen full rights to carry out their agenda.

Despite their intense efforts to secure papal approval, they were in no rush to recruit their head inquisitors and it took two years for them to name the men that were to lead the carnage that was to come. Miguel de Morillo and Juan de San Martin were assigned as inquisitors in Seville on 27 September 1480 and they wasted no time in beginning their purge; by the end of 1480, a significant number of conversos had fled Seville, in trepidation of what lay ahead on the horizon.

Their fear for their lives would be proved right when, in February 1481, the first public execution of heretics took place. They called it *auto-da-fé*, or Act of Faith; six people who had been accused of heresy were burnt alive on the stake as a public demonstration of the fate that awaited those who were not fully converted to the Catholic faith.

The Inquisition continued to escalate when, in February 1482, Pope Sixtus IV appointed seven additional inquisitors to cover the other territories outside Seville, no doubt under the same threat of military retraction from King Ferdinand. By 1483, the Inquisition had spread out into the neighbouring regions of Aragon, Valencia and Catalonia.

To cope with the increased workload, the infamous Tomas de Torquemada was hired as grand inquisitor. Ironically, Torquemada was the descendant of a Jewish grandmother who had converted to Catholicism. She would have, no doubt, been considered a conversos had she been alive during the Inquisition. Bizarrely, many members of the Spanish royal family were also of Jewish ancestry, including King Ferdinand, who allegedly beat his wife, Queen Isabella, when on one occasion she dared to discuss his bloodline.

Torquemada was a sadistic and fanatical friar who brought a new level of brutality to the Inquisition. He had the upper hand on other inquisitors as he had been a close friend and the confessor of Queen Isabella I since her childhood. He was a great influence over the queen and this gave him full authority and power over his victims throughout the fifteen years he was in control. He and his co-inquisitors took the rampage to a new level. They set up their first tribunal in Cordoba and, before long, they extended into other cities across Spain.

As investigations were carried out, witnesses gathered to give evidence against their Jewish, Moorish or otherwise suspicious neighbours. The inquisition's primary focus appeared to be on Jews, but it did not hold back when it came to targeting Muslims, Protestants and other Christian cults that were not strictly a part of the Catholic Church.

Evidence of any kind was acceptable, such as the lack of smoke from the chimney of a Jewish household on a Saturday, which would be interpreted as a sign that the inhabitants were honouring Sabbath. Proof of heresy could also be found in a person who was seen speaking to a suspected heretic, or simply buying extra vegetables before a Jewish Passover day. And it most definitely would be applied to any person who demonstrated behaviour that could be construed to be linked with witchcraft, sodomy or freemasonry.

To enforce his tyranny, Torquemada published a set of guidelines that Catholics were to use to identify a Jewish converso:

> If you see that your neighbours are wearing clean and fancy clothes on Saturdays, they are Jews. If they clean their houses on Fridays and light candles earlier than usual on that night, they are Jews. If they eat unleavened bread and begin their meals with celery and lettuce during Holy Week, they are Jews. If they say prayers facing a wall, bowing back and forth, they are Jews.

All denunciations were anonymous. This resulted in a number of suspects being falsely accused by jealous rivals or personal enemies, who used the Inquisition's incentives as a means to advance their wealth or status.

Those accused had little to no chance of mounting a defence, as the name of their accuser or the witnesses who testified against them were not divulged to them or their defence attorneys. Trials were well organised and meticulous notes were taken, giving the process a false appearance of sophistication and fairness. But, in truth, the accused did not stand a chance. Even their advocates were bound by so many rules they could not effectively defend their clients, particularly as in most instances, their client would have been forced to confess their guilt under extreme duress.

It is no coincidence that the term 'Spanish inquisition' is synonymous with torture. Men, women and children under suspicion of heresy were subjected to torment and horrendous physical torture during interrogations with the aim of forcing a confession. Some were pardoned in exchange for confession and penance, but others were condemned to a horrific death at the stake. Even when all hope was lost, and they were faced with the punishment of death, the innocent 'heretics' had two choices: confess and die by strangulation, or stay true to their faith and burn alive.

It is estimated that, between 1481 and 1488, 700 Jews were handed over to the Inquisition, a significant number of which were burnt at the stake. A further 5,000 were allowed back into the Catholic Church in exchange for penances.

Although the Jews were not the sole victims of the Spanish inquisition, it became apparent to Pope Sixtus IV that they formed the majority of those accused. With growing concern that they were being targeted because of their race, he wrote a letter to King Ferdinand and Queen Isabella, to remind them that the Inquisition was in place to tackle heresy all together, not to target one particular religion or race that could be prone to heresy.

However, his words fell on deaf ears and the inquisitors carried on with their quest. The Pope, still afraid to anger the Spanish rulers, did not seek to take further action and left them the power to continue what they had started. After all, the Inquisition was financially profitable for both sides. In Spain, the wealth and property of any condemned heretic would be confiscated and added to the royal treasury. And the Church would profit substantially, not only from Spain's military support, but from the desperation of accused heretics, who were given the option to pay a hefty fee in exchange for a papal pardon, should they wish to escape punishment and death .

Some of the residents of Spain, however, were not prepared to accept the seemingly limitless control that the inquisitors had over them. On 14 September 1485, inquisitor Pedro Arbues was making his way from his house in Zaragoza towards his local cathedral to join in matins. Aware that the torture and terror he had inflicted on the local community made him a potential target for an act of revenge, he wore a coat of mail beneath his robes. He also wore a steel skull-cap beneath his hat and carried a bludgeon. But all the precautions he took served to be of no use when two men closed in on him and murdered him as he began his prayers.

They could not have picked a more prolific victim. As Arbues was one of Queen Isabella's personal confessors, she ensured that such an act of defiance would be used in her political war against the heretics. The two murderers suffered an excruciating death and she erected a monument, dedicated to Arbues, on which she wrote, 'Because of his zeal he became hateful to the Jews; by whom slain, he fell here a martyr in the year 1485.'

The population of Zaragoza would also pay for his death. They were considered traitors and treated with suspicion, simply for being residents of the doomed city. Many deserted the town; however, no matter how far they travelled, at times it was not enough, as the son of Gaspar de Santa Cruz would find out. Cruz fled Zaragoza just after Arbues' murder and started a new life in the hope of raising his family without the stigma of their origins. He died a happy man and was buried with dignity. However, when the inquisitors fell upon his family and discovered their origins, they arrested his son and made him read out a script publically condemning his own father for the sole crime of having resided in a city that was, in their eyes, condemned. Then, they took him to his father's grave, where he was ordered to dig up his corpse and burn it under the watchful eye of an inquisitor. He had no choice but to comply; if he did not destroy the grave of his beloved father, he would pay with his life.

The most popular methods of torture that the Inquisition used were *garrucha*, *toca* and *potro*. The inquisitors were officially forbidden from permanently harming or drawing blood during their investigations, but they were resourceful and used methods of torture that appeared to be within those boundaries. If they did surpass them, the Catholic Church had ruled that they could confess and be forgiven by another inquisitor; therefore, there were no real boundaries as to how far they could go in their mission to cleanse their flock. Torture was carried out by the local public executioner in the presence of the inquisitor and a doctor.

The application of *garrucha* was one of the more popular methods. The suspect's ankles would be bound and their hands tied behind their back. They would then be hoisted about six feet in the air with a rope attached to their wrists that ran through a pulley. Weights would often be attached to their feet and they would then be left suspended for as long as it was deemed necessary. If the inquisitors did not get the result that they wanted, the suspect would be dropped suddenly, exerting immense strain on their arms and legs, which often resulted in dislocation or torn ligaments.

The second method, the *toca*, involved stuffing a cloth into the mouth of the suspect and spilling water forcibly into their mouth with a jug or funnel so that the victim felt as if they were drowning. Often, they would block the nasal air passage to increase the pain, resulting in burst blood vessels.

The third was the most frequently used. This was the *potro*—more commonly known as the rack. The suspect would be tied to a wooden frame with chains attached to their ankles and wrists. They would then be pulled in both directions through a network of pulleys and rollers that would stretch them apart, tearing their joints and muscles to the extent required. This could leave the victim an invalid or result in death if taken to the extreme.

William Lithgow, a Scottish traveller and writer, described in great detail the torture he went through when he was subjected to all three methods of torture by the Spanish Inquisition after being detained in Spain on suspicion of being a spy. In his book, *Rare Adventures and Painful Peregrinations*, he tells of how he was subjected to the *garrucha* during which his sinews and his knees were crushed. He was then strapped to the *potro* and was racked before being subjected to the third ordeal, the *toca*.

> [...] the tormentor went to an earthen jar standing full of water, a little beneath my head; from when carrying a pot full of water, in the bottom whereof there was an incised hole, which being stopped by his thumb, till it came to my mouth, he did pour it in my belly; the measure being a Spanish sombre which is an English pottle; the first and second devices I gladly received, such was the scorching drought of my tormenting pain, and likewise I had drunk none for three days before. But afterward, at the third charge perceiving these measures of water to be inflicted on me as tortures, O strangling tortures! I closed my lips again-standing that eager crudelity. Whereat the governor of the prison enraged, set my teeth asunder with a pair of iron cadges, detaining them there, at every several turn, both mainly and manually whereupon my hunger-clunged belly waxing great, grew drum-like imbolstred, for it being a suffocating pain, in regard of my head hanging downward, and the water reingorging itself, in my throat, with a struggling force, it strangled and swallowed up my breath from yowling and groaning.

Torture was not always administered. At times, just the threat of torture was enough to crack the toughest conversos. They controlled the masses through fear, ensuring that there was always an element of secrecy to their judicial trials and torture sessions, which often took place behind closed doors. The fear of the unknown can be more powerful than any torture and they effectively used that to their advantage. A state of deep paranoia spread across the country. Non-Catholic Spanish residents lived with the fear that they would be denounced by just about anyone that they were connected with, even more so when it was made known that accused heretics could have their punishment reduced if they denounced other heretics in their area.

In 1492, and under advice by Torquemada, Ferdinand issued the Alhambra decree, an Edict of Expulsion ordering all Jews to leave Spain or face the death penalty. The Jews tried to bribe Ferdinand, offering him 30,000 ducats to leave them be. Rabbi Abarbanel delivered the bribe to the King and Queen himself. He dropped to his knees and wept before them, begging them to accept the offer and take pity on his fellow Jews. Ferdinand considered his request and was on the verge of accepting, when Torquemada dramatically barged into the royal court carrying a crucifix. Furious, he slammed the cross down on the table and said to Ferdinand, 'Judas Iscariot sold Christ for 30 pieces of silver. Your Highness is about to sell him for 30,000 ducats. Here he is. Take him and sell him.' It was a bold and dangerous move, but one that persuaded Ferdinand to change his mind and go through with the decree.

According to some estimates, 50,000 Jews were forced to convert to the Catholic faith to avoid being exiled from Spain, while up to 40,000 Jews fled the country, leaving all their wealth behind as the decree banned them from exporting money, silver or gold. Most fled into surrounding countries, but a large portion moved to Portugal, unaware that the inquisition would eventually reach their new homeland as well.

The small details that we can gather from these exoduses would break the heart of even the hardest of souls. Travel was gruelling in those times and many died of starvation, exhaustion or disease whist *en route* to a life that they believed would be better. Even if they reached their intended destination, they had no idea what would be waiting for them there. Some were murdered in inhospitable lands that they travelled through, while others were taken as slaves.

Survivors told tragic tales. One in particular describes a family who had been travelling on a ship that was filled to the brim with exiles. When a plague broke out, the captain of the ship docked near a deserted island and ordered them all to leave the ship, abandoning them to certain death. Wandering aimlessly in search for help that did not exist, a wife carried her two infants as her husband led them down a sandy pathway. Suffering extreme exhaustion, the husband collapsed by the side of the trail. When he awoke some time later, he discovered that his children had died of hunger and, inconsolable, he buried them in the sand. He and his wife never made it off the island.

It is believed that this decree was issued as much for religious purposes as financial. Spain had just defeated the Muslims in Grenada, and claimed back the last territory that they occupied in the Iberian Peninsula. The war was costly and they needed to rebuild their economy. The quickest way was to force the Jews and other conversos, some of whom were very wealthy, to leave and then claim the assets that they had no choice but to leave behind. Those who converted and remained were automatically thrown under suspicion as their conversion was thought to be insincere. The Jews could not win—if they did not convert they were killed, and if they did convert they were investigated anyway and often put to death if the slightest rumour came out.

Torquemada became such a hated figure throughout Spain that he had to be assigned 300 soldiers to protect him as he went about his inquisition. The methods of torture became even more creative; there must have been an extraordinarily perverse mind behind them. Sponsored by the Catholic Church, a wide variety of tools were created to win this battle against the poison that they believed was rotting their country. Judas cradles were used—an iron pyramid that a naked suspect would be suspended above, dangling from ropes only to be lowered onto it, piercing the anus to whatever depth and width required. It was a barbaric and inhumane method of torture, designed to create the maximum amount of pain whilst not actually causing death. There is also rumour that they used the Iron Virgin. A large, hollow iron doll that would open at the back and the suspect would be placed inside. Its inner wall would be covered in long spikes so that, when it was shut, the victim's body would be punctured in multiple areas. Smaller tools of torture were also used to inflict disfiguration and pain on the ankles, feet and fingers.

The Inquisition was at its worst from 1480 to 1510 and was finally abolished in 1834 during the reign of Queen Isabella II. The estimated figures surrounding the Inquisition vary immensely from one historian to another, but recent sources conclude that, between 1550 and 1800, approximately 150,000 trials were carried out and 3,000 heretics were put to death.

Torquemada died of poor health in 1498, putting an end to his fifteen-year career as the greatest terrorist of the Spanish inquisition. Prior to his death, Pope Alexander VI sent four of his own inquisitors to Rome to investigate complaints against Torquemada but, predictably, nothing came of it. After all, the Catholic Church had benefited immensely from his actions as grand inquisitor, both financially and politically. He was buried in a monastery in Avila, but his grave was ransacked by rioters in 1832 and his bones were incinerated in a mock *auto-da-fé*. In some way, the rioters must have felt that this was the only way they could now serve justice to the man who had haunted their dreams and destroyed their lives.

For many years, the Vatican kept its archives relating to the Inquisitions a well-guarded secret. But eventually, in 1998, they released the records on a limited basis. Since, there have been conflicting opinions and versions of what actually took place. Some academics who have seen the records are now claiming that the stories passed down through the centuries are highly exaggerated and are but myths spread by Protestant monks and Jewish scholars as propaganda against the Catholic Church. Each side has their own numbers, with historic tales telling us that hundreds of thousands were tortured and killed, and the other side claiming that hardly any deaths occurred as a result of the Inquisition. They even go further to say that it was all a very well-run programme with rules and limitations on torture methods, and that the Inquisition prisons were far better than the regular prisons in Spain at that time.

Unless I am able to travel back through history, I cannot say with certainty which version is correct, but I am swayed by the following unanswered questions. Why did the Catholic Church withhold the archives for so many centuries if there was nothing scandalous to find within their pages? Particularly bearing in mind the pressure that the Church has been under in the last century to account for its past actions, surely these records would have put a stop to what Catholic authorities claimed were wild speculation and myths? Why is it that so many incidents and stories that have been passed through history all appear to corroborate the version we have always known, and yet the Vatican archives tell a much more acceptable account?

However, what sways me even further are the other instances in history when the Catholic Church has done just that; other times, when fanatical church leaders oppressed their flock and used violence and torture to control them or force them into converting to their religion.

The Vatican still runs by the Canon law, which is a book of regulations that serves as a guide to the leadership of the Church. Despite many reviews of this charter over the last centuries, they have chosen to retain a law that supported the Inquisition. The law in question is Canon 1311:

> The Church has an innate and proper right to coerce offending members of the Christian faithful by means of papal sanction.

The terrible Inquisition is, for most, a story of the past...but is it really? With this law still in place, is the world still at risk of such acts of torture and murder occurring again?

From 1941 to 1945, the Orthodox Serbs in Croatia and Bosnia were persecuted, tortured and killed if they refused to convert to the Catholic religion. According to the US Holocaust Memorial Museum, it is estimated that the Ustaša authorities murdered approximately 335,000 ethnic Serb residents in Bosnia and Croatia during the period of Ustaše rule, out of which nearly 50,000 were murdered in the Jasenovac concentration camp. The Vatican was fully aware of the plans to convert ethnic-Serbs to Roman Catholicism and Catholic priests took part directly in the atrocities. I will leave it to the reader to form an opinion.

CHAPTER 5

Thugs:
Killers And Thieves

Have you ever wondered where the term 'thug' comes from? Today we think of a violent person, but its true origin dates back to the thirteenth century when a group of criminals, known as thugs, terrorised the population of India over an extended period. In Hindi, the word *thuggee* represents the acts of theft and murder that these criminals carried out, which earned them that infamous title.

It is hard to assess just how long the thugs were in operation as their existence was only fully uncovered in the late eighteenth and early nineteenth centuries, when India's occupying British government decided to launch an investigation into a phenomenon that was taking place in rural areas throughout the country. A number of travellers had gone missing in the past few years and, after collecting data from several regions, it appeared that these disappearances had been going on much longer than they had initially thought.

The reason these crimes had gone undetected was because they had occurred in so many different locations at a time when communication was not all that efficient. No connection was ever made and, in most cases, the missing persons were assumed to have fallen victim to thieves on their travels, a regular occurrence in this poverty-stricken nation.

The British would not have been so concerned had all the disappearances consisted of lone travellers or vagabonds as it was expected that, in such a poor country, opportunists were prepared to kill for just about anything. But entire caravans of travellers, containing at times large numbers of people, seemed to be vanishing without a trace. As further reports came in, they feared that whoever was behind the crimes may be far more dangerous than they realised.

Clearly, theft was not the villains' sole motivation. Had it been, they could have simply restrained their victims and taken their spoils. But it appeared that they were taking their time to kill their victims and hide their bodies. In most instances, those who disappeared were never seen again, dead or alive, which forced investigators to presume that all those who were missing had been murdered.

By the early 1830s, the data they had collected brought them to the realisation that the numbers were far higher than they could have possibly imagined, with thousands of disappearances in the past decade alone. They also noticed that a secretive group called 'thugs' was regularly mentioned in reports and testimonies.

The British Governor-General of India, Lord William Bentinck, requested that a taskforce be set up with the mission to uncover the workings of this group of thieves. They called it 'The Thugs Department'. As they collected witness testimonies, they discovered that what appeared to be a cluster of rogue gangs was, in fact, an organised network of highly trained criminals who operated in separate clans all over the country. The taskforce also realised that this was not a new trend; the thugs appeared to have been functioning for thousands of years, although there were no means of determining just how long they had been active. What they did know was that these groups consisted of professional, disciplined assassins who preyed on innocent families and tradesmen that they had selected as targets. They were extremely organised, with clever tactics that had been developed over the centuries, and they appeared to be active in many locations around the country.

It would not be an easy job for the British. The thugs had survived for so long due to their ability to mask their identities and integrate into regular society without attracting suspicion. They were so secretive that even their wives and relatives often had no inclination whatsoever of their involvement in the group. Even though society in India at that time was divided into strict castes that did not mix, the thugs' membership group included men from all social levels. United by a mysterious bond, street vendors worked hand-in-hand with wealthy merchants and bankers. It was even rumoured that relatives of the Indian royal family were involved.

British civil servant William Sleeman was a stern, middle-aged man from Cornwall, who had been working on the taskforce since its creation. He had been one of the first to insist that the issue was greater than the British government initially wanted to admit. Unlike the majority of his colleagues, he was genuinely fascinated with India and its culture; he had studied its religious and social complexities and spoke fluent Hindi. He was a highly intelligent man who used investigation techniques that were unheard of at that time, such as profiling and using information gathered from previous attacks to predict the location of the next one. He increased military presence in key areas and publically announced that they were prepared to offer 'king's evidence' status to those who wished to break their silence and denounce their brothers in crime. By coming forward and agreeing to testify, they would escape the death penalty. It was an irresistible offer to a handful of thugs, who promptly handed themselves in.

Once arrested, they appeared to be more than willing to not only co-operate, but also give up their brothers in crime. At first, Sleeman was suspicious of this, particularly because of their deceitful nature; eventually, however, he realised it was their undying belief in fate that was behind their actions. They were convinced that their destiny, and that of their colleagues, had been decided long in advance and, hence, to betray their identities would not change it either way.

Once Sleeman had several prisoners, he was able to piece together their hidden world of gruesome murders and dark rituals. He began by questioning one man, Feringhea, who was the head of a thug gang. After he convinced him to turn king's evidence, Feringhea gave up the names of his gang members and led Sleeman to a mass grave hidden in a mango grove. To his horror, the grave contained nearly 100 bodies at various stages of decomposition.

There was a snowball effect from there; with each arrest came more confessions and the names of additional thugs were revealed. Mass graves were uncovered across the country and, as they exhumed the bodies, they discovered something that they found deeply disturbing. Although they now knew that they were dealing with a large network of criminals, they were baffled when a comparison of crime reports from different locations concluded that all the victims had been killed in exactly the same manner: by strangulation. It seemed very strange that a band of thieves would choose a method of killing that required more time and physical effort than simply using a knife or machete. But, more importantly, no regular gang of thieves would all use an identical method of killing unless there was a very sinister reason for it.

Sleeman took a hands-on approach and regularly accompanied his men on journeys to locate graves, collect information and interrogate suspects. Often, his young French wife accompanied them as they trekked across the country. They braved torrential monsoon rains and scorching heat, breeze-whipped coasts and dense jungles, all the while avoiding poisonous insects and fearsome rainforest beasts. His wife shared his zeal of putting to an end the thug threat; they were on a mission and were prepared to face anything to complete it.

With mounds of incoming information, a clearer picture began to emerge. The thugs were well and truly a nationwide Hindu cult that operated in separate clans, but who all had the same fundamental beliefs and practices. The clans often included several generations of men from the same family, as fathers would recruit their own offspring and train them from a young age. They would allow them to become progressively involved in the killings from the age of ten, first as spectators and gradually as participants from their teenage years.

Hence, most clans were composed of relatives or families whose ancestors had formed strong bonds through generations of thieving and killing together.

They were also far better organised than the British had initially thought, with a hierarchy that was more of a democracy than a dictatorship. Each clan had a leader known as the *jemadar*, who was usually the clan member with the most experience. Because of his knowledge, the *jemadar* would be responsible for training new members and had more influence in the decision-making within the group. New recruits had to strive to attain the first rank in the cult which was called *bhurtote*, meaning strangler, and then could work their way up the hierarchy until their death. In the world of thugs, membership was a lifelong commitment. The cult became their family and they even had their own language, *Ramasee*, which was based on Hindi but was incomprehensible to anyone outside the group.

Sleeman went on to discover how this cult was able to make large groups of travellers disappear without a trace. Each time, the cult's process was the same and began with choosing their victims. They picked their prey very carefully, which was one reason why they were able to operate for such a long period without being caught. They avoided high profile families and only attacked travellers that were far from their home so that their absence would not be noticed until weeks later, giving them time to erase all trace of their attack. They stalked travellers who were visiting their area to assess whether they could potentially be their next victims, and they relied on religious omens to confirm that they had chosen the right prey.

Next, they would infiltrate the group of travellers under the pretence that they were looking for safety in numbers, a regular practice in those times. Often, lone travellers or small groups would team up with larger groups that they met along the way as, the higher numbers they travelled in, the less risk there was of attack by thieves. Depending on the size of the group, they would send one or more of their professional assassins to infiltrate the caravan of travellers. If more than one thug was to infiltrate, they would send them into the group a few days apart to avoid any suspicion that the new arrivals were connected. Once inside, the killers would earn the trust of the group by being very helpful and charming towards its key members. Then, they would wait until they reached a location that was isolated enough for them to carry out the attack without being seen or heard. It could take weeks to set up a large attack as more men had to be infiltrated into the group, which meant more time was needed for the hapless travellers to lower their guard.

Once they were ready to strike, the most senior thugs present would give the signal, which was usually done by saying to the others 'bring the tobacco'. They would then carry out a surprise attack, either at night or during periods of rest when their victims were dozing beneath the tropical trees and were completely off guard. To suffocate their victims they used rope, their turban cloth or, more commonly, the *rumal,* a yellow sash which they tied around their waist. The strangulations were often carried out by a trio of thugs. The first would run his cloth around the victim's neck while the other two would lift him by his lower limbs and slam him into the ground, where he would be held down until he died.

They would slaughter every single traveller in the group, as it was in their code of honour to never allow their prey to escape their fate. Women and children rarely travelled far in those times but, if they were present, they too would be killed.

Each member of the clan had a very specific role to play at each stage of the attack, from the infiltration to the actual killings. It was a well-oiled machine that had been running for far too long, terrorising the natives countrywide.

As the thug taskforce made arrests and began to carry out executions, they were given the answer to another mystery that had disturbed them throughout the investigation. Why were the victims killed in the same way? They discovered it was all part of a religious ritual that involved a barbaric practice that, even in those days, was considered to be long lost in history: human sacrifices.

The victims were killed to be given as a blood offering to the powerful Hindi goddess Kali, who they considered to be the goddess of violence and death. Referred to as 'the black one', this fearsome goddess is often pictured as a dark-skinned female with four arms and long, tangled hair. Her eyes are crimson red and her long tongue hangs out between her fangs, as if she is panting for a taste of blood. She wears lavish gold jewellery speckled with precious stones. Around her neck hangs a string of human heads tinged with blood and she wears a skirt of human arms around her waist. In one hand she holds a blood-stained machete and, in the other, a severed head still dripping with blood. She stands defiantly with her left foot on the chest of a man, said to be the God Shiva, who lies dead in the blood-stained earth.

She was considered to be a very powerful goddess who craved human blood, and the thugs worshipped her with fanatical devotion, convinced that they were her children and had been created by her sweat. They believed that Kali would become enraged and kill mankind if she was not kept satisfied with endless offerings of blood. They killed their victims by strangulation as they did not want to risk wasting even one drop of the blood that was intended as an offering to their goddess.

Sleeman's account provides the dark mythology behind their belief in Kali.

Once upon a time the world was infested with a monstrous demon named Rukt

Bij-dana, who devoured mankind as fast as they were created. So gigantic was his stature that the deepest pools of the ocean reached no higher than his waist. This horrid prodigy Kali cut in twain with her sword, but from every drop of blood that fell to the ground there sprang a new demon. For some reason she went on destroying them, till the hellish brood multiplied so fast that she waxed hot and weary with her endless task. She paused for a while, and, from the sweat brushed off one of her arms, she created two men, to whom she gave a rumal, or handkerchief, and commanded them to strangle the demons. When they had slain them all, they offered to return the rumal, but the goddess bade them keep it and transmit it to their posterity, with the injunction to destroy all men who were not of their kindred.

A tradition is current among thugs, that about the period of the commencement of the Kali Yug, Kali co-operated with them so far as to relieve them of the trouble of interring the dead bodies, by devouring them herself. On one occasion, after destroying a traveller, the body, as usual, was left unburied; and a novice, unguardedly looking behind him, saw the naked goddess in the act of feasting upon it, half of it hanging out of her mouth. She, upon this, declared that she would no longer devour those whom the thugs slaughtered, but she condescended to present them with one of her teeth for a pickaxe, a rib for a knife, and the hem of her lower garment for a noose, and ordered them, for the future, to cut and bury the bodies of whom they destroyed.

Once they had murdered all their victims, the thugs would carry out a macabre ritual in honour of Kali, during which they would offer her the blood of the victims. Then they would set about getting rid of the bodies and all evidence of the attack.

The thugs were masters at covering up their crimes, which enabled them to operate for thousands of years without detection. They buried their victims in mass graves, often breaking their limbs and cutting deep gashes into their flesh to accelerate decomposition. After they had buried the bodies and performed a final ritual, they would carry out a clean-up operation. To hide the overturned ground, they would often scatter shrubbery, waste and litter across the dusty soil to make it appear as if a group of travellers had camped and then went on their way. The thugs would then divide their belongings, livestock and money, ensuring they kept a portion to be offered to Kali to appease her.

Once Sleeman had pieced together their *modus operandi,* he decided to use it against them and he sent a teams of elite officers disguised as travellers and tradesmen to key locations where he knew that they would have a high chance of being targeted by the cult killers. Only this time, the predator would become the prey. As the thugs prepared to launch their ritualistic attacks, their seemingly defenceless victims would reveal their true identities, surround them and take them prisoner.

The trap worked on quite a few occasions and this success led to Sleeman's promotion to superintendent in 1835. He continued his campaign to annihilate the thugs and made steady progress, despite some resistance in certain regions. Incredibly, the thugs appeared to have a few supporters who, out of fear of the goddess Kali, would hide cult members who were on the run or, worse yet, kill the soldiers who were hunting them down. By 1839, the core structure of thugs had collapsed and Sleeman was promoted to commissioner. His operation led to the imprisonment or hanging of nearly 1,500 thugs, including clan leader, Behram, who had killed nearly a thousand victims by his own hand using his turban cloth. During his interrogation, Sleeman asked Behram if he felt remorse for luring his victims with pretence and then killing them in cold blood. He replied that he most certainly did not and compared thugs to hunters of large game, describing the thrill of stalking and finally killing their victims as the same emotion that a hunter feels when he has overcome his prey.

Judge Curwen Smith, who presided over most of the thug trials, was so appalled by the brutal nature of the cult's members that he wrote the following in a letter to Lord Bentinck:

> In all my experience in the judicial line for upwards of twenty years I have never heard of such atrocities or presided over such trials, such cold-blooded murder, such heart-rending scenes of distress and misery, such base ingratitude, such total abandonment of every principle which binds man to man, which softens the heart and elevates mankind above the brute creation.

Even at their moment of death, the thugs were unrepentant. They are said to have been utterly calm and emotionless, asking only if they could place the cord around their own neck before they were hanged.

Eventually, the cult was crushed and, at the end of the nineteenth century, the British government declared them to be officially extinguished. The people of India were free from these religious mass murderers, who lurked in every corner of the country and had inflicted terror over them for thousands of years. Unfortunately, Sleeman did not live to see that day; after forty years of combat against this killer cult, he died of a heart attack on his way home to England. But his legacy carries on and he will always be known as the determined officer who exposed the thugs for what they truly were and brought their organised operation to its knees.

In modern Hinduism, the Goddess Kali represents empowerment and the understanding of life and death. She bears no resemblance to the cruel goddess of thugs, who appears to have been a reinvented version of the original deity. To this day, some still argue that religion was an insignificant part of the cult and instead view them as rogue mass murderers who stole and killed out of greed.

But it is highly unlikely that a regular group of thieves would have lasted for so many years over numerous generations. There had to be a stronger glue than mere greed and, judging by the number of murders and the identical ritual in which they killed their victims, there is no doubt in my mind that they were a religious cult that carried out human sacrifices for their goddess.

If theft was their primary motivation, they would have killed quickly and then fled the scene, leaving the bodies behind. But they did not. Instead, they took their time and meticulously studied their victims and planned each attack in advance. They spent days, at times even weeks, integrating with the caravan of travellers before carrying out a series of rituals and ceremonies before and after the killings. This very much demonstrates the fact that religious motivation was the driving force behind the killings, while the theft was a bonus.

To add to that, a number of the thugs had no need to thieve as they had good occupations and some were even rather wealthy. They would not have been involved in such a dangerous hobby unless they had a strong belief that their goddess required it. After all, the thugs must have felt that, by keeping the goddess Kali content, they were in some way saving humanity from death. What is rather strange is the fact that, although the majority of thug members were Hindu, there were also a number of Sheikh and Muslim members who had incorporated the worship of Kali into their religion. They, too, despite contradictions with their own religion, must have felt some sense of duty to protect their families by carrying out these rituals.

But, no matter how they viewed it, the facts speak for themselves and there is no elegant way to portray a group of conniving and cold-hearted killers. They perfected their art over generations and certainly lived up to their violent name by carrying out the longest-lasting killing spree in history.

Outside of India, the story of these thugs is little known, despite the use of their name in British vocabulary to describe the lowest criminal outcasts of society. Perhaps the fate that they so believed in has found them unfit to be remembered.

CHAPTER 6

The Family:
Charles Manson

'Pig'

The word had been painted in blood across the front door of 10050 Cielo Drive, Los Angeles. Inside, the lifeless body of a heavily pregnant woman was one of four found on the property. Lying in a pool of blood, the beautiful actress was barely recognisable. Who was behind such a horrific crime? As the story hit news headlines worldwide, local police authorities were on a mission to find out.

Thirty-five years earlier, on 12 November 1934, sixteen-year-old teenager Kathleen Maddox gave birth to a boy in Cincinnati, Ohio. It was an unplanned and unwanted pregnancy that came about as the result of a drunken fling with military colonel, Walter Scott. Maddox came from a religious and violent household. To escape her mother's beatings, the young girl turned to a life of alcohol abuse and promiscuity, often running away from home and disappearing for days at a time.

For several weeks, Maddox called her son 'no name Maddox' until finally settling for Charles Milles Maddox. When she married William Manson a few months later, Charles was given his last name which he retained for the rest of his life, despite the short duration of their marriage.

Maddox's alcohol abuse escalated when she found herself single again. When intoxicated, she became uncontrollable, often landing in trouble with police or putting herself in dangerous situations. On one occasion, she sold baby Manson to a childless waitress for the price of a jug of beer, but fortunately her brother found out and returned to the bar to retrieve him.

The rest of Manson's childhood was miserable. At five years of age he was sent to live with relatives in West Virginia when his mother was incarcerated for theft. When she was released three years later they were reunited, only for the young boy to become entangled in the chaos of her lifestyle. They lived like vagabonds for several years; Maddox prostituted herself to fund her addictions and they stayed in run-down motel rooms in crime-ridden areas. Manson became a child of the streets from the age of eight, keeping company with drug addicts and homeless drunks in his area.

At the age of thirteen his mother handed him over to social services to be placed into foster care but just ten months later he escaped the Gibault School for Boys in Indiana and turned up on her doorstep, begging her to take him back. She refused, leaving Manson no other choice but to fend for himself on the streets. His freedom was short lived. He was arrested for theft shortly after and spent time in several juvenile centres before being sent to a reform school in Indiana.

For four years the school became his home. According to his own account, it was a house of horrors where he and other children were tortured and raped by the guards and older children, which led him to escape at seventeen years of age. He fled to Utah where he again turned to crime, resulting in his arrest for car theft and robbery. This time he was sent to a federal prison, where a year into his stay, he sodomised a fellow inmate while holding a razor blade to his throat. Manson later claimed that he had been subjected to homosexual assaults and beatings during his stay in this facility. He was eventually transferred to the high security Federal Reformatory in Chillicothe, Ohio, where he was given the opportunity to progress with his schooling. Despite having an IQ of 121, Manson was illiterate and his education was equal to that of a nine year old. Studying appeared to have a positive effect on him and by 1954 he had progressed to the level of a twelve year old.

After a couple of years of impeccable behaviour, he was released on parole. He married Rosalie Willis and before long they were expecting their first child. But Manson could not stay away from trouble and he turned to theft once more to supplement his low income. He was convicted of car theft for the second time and was sent to a jail in California. During his incarceration, his wife gave birth to their son, Charles Junior. For the first year she and her son visited Manson regularly, but then she began a relationship with another man and the visits dwindled until they ceased all together.

In late 1958, Manson was released on parole and sure enough, his life of crime was reignited. Theft, drug dealing, pimping and cheque forgery were among the criminal activities that landed him back in jail. During his brief period of freedom he had married a prostitute, Candy Stevens, who claimed that she was pregnant with his child. He showed no interest in fatherhood which led Stevens to divorce him shortly after the birth of their son, Charles Luther.

In 1961, Manson was transferred to the US Penitentiary on McNeil Island where he befriended notorious gang leader Alvin 'Creepy' Karpis. The crime lord taught him to play the steel guitar and introduced him to other prisoners who had showbiz connections. It was the start of Manson's obsession with the world of music stars and celebrities.

When his parole hearing took place in March 1967, Manson was in his early thirties and had been institutionalised for the majority of his life. During his hearing, he begged the parole board to allow him to stay in prison. After all, the outside world had become an alien environment to him whereas life in jail was one that he knew well and had become comfortable with. To his dismay, the parole committee denied his request. Unbeknownst to them, they had just released a very dangerous man into a society that was radically changing and was filled with naive youngsters who were ripe for the picking.

Manson moved into a small apartment in San Francisco, where the Hippy Revolution was in full swing. The air was thick with Peace and Love vibes emanating from free-spirited youths that congregated and expressed their rejection of normal society by flaunting their uninhibited practices of free sex, drugs and frugal material possessions. The Summer of Love attracted thousands of young hippy drifters to San Francisco. Flower power tunes blared out as couples made love in the open and strangers, high on 'love' (drugs) hugged energetically and swapped clothes. Lost and confused souls were united on a crusade to find a higher purpose, a path to enlightenment. It was the perfect hunting ground for wannabe gurus and fanatic extremists, resulting in many cults and alternative groups being formed during this period. Manson saw an opportunity and took it.

He moved in with his new girlfriend, Mary Brunner and soon after they had a child, Valentine. Manson had complete control over Brunner, who stayed at home with their son while he strived to establish himself as a guru among the clusters of hippies that were moving through the city. His charismatic personality and intense demeanour soon lured in his first disciples, who were all female. Manson moved them into his marital home and before long his community, which he called 'The Family', comprised of eighteen women.

The self-proclaimed prophet filled his follower's minds with dark doctrines that were based on satanic beliefs and theories from Scientology, both of which he'd studied during his time in prison. But his seduction didn't end there. With a cocktail of powerful drugs, music and mystical speeches, he seduced his devoted disciples and used sex as a tool to control them. The group became his harem and the women within were so deeply obsessed with him that they were prepared to go to any lengths to please him.

Towards the end of that summer, Manson bought an old school bus which they painted with bright rainbow colours, before setting off on a series of road trips. They crossed state lines, recruiting followers along the way, and it was around this time that his infamous 'Helter Skelter' doctrine began to form. He told his followers that a racial war was imminent and that they would need to make preparations to face it; it was the seedling that he would later develop into a Beatles-inspired message of doom.

It was in late spring of 1968 that Manson met *The Beach Boys* singer Dennis Wilson. It all began when Wilson picked up two female hitchhikers who he invited back to his house to freshen up, before continuing their journey. But when he returned home after a late night at his recording studio, he was astounded to find that Manson and twelve of his followers had moved into his house. Being the master manipulator that he was, Manson managed to convince Wilson to let them stay and together they practised their music, exchanged ideas and enjoyed the attentive services of the cult's women, who made themselves available for sex at any time of day or night. Manson kept the women dosed up on powerful drugs such as LSD, which made them compliant and allowed him to control them fully.

Dennis introduced Manson to several contacts in the music industry, including Gregg Jakobson, who was impressed with his musical talent and funded the use of a recording studio. Manson took this as a sign that he was going to break the music industry and become a worldwide star. But the dream soon ended when, after a few months, Wilson reached the end of his tether. Supporting over a dozen squatters was taking its toll financially and he was no longer content with the living arrangements. He asked The Family to leave, whereupon they moved to Spahn's Movie Ranch in California.

It was a large ranch that had been used as a movie set for old Western movies, but which was now in very poor condition. The eighty-year-old owner of the ranch, George Spahn, was blind and unable to make any improvements around the property. He made a deal with Manson; he would allow The Family to live on the ranch for free if they did renovation work and cleaned the place up.

It was the perfect location for this increasingly bizarre cult. Away from prying eyes and with plenty of room to accommodate them, they could practise their alternative lifestyle in peace. To keep Spahn happy, Manson ordered his female followers to assist him with daily tasks and service him sexually. It was around this time that Manson recruited several male followers, including Charles Watson. Nicknamed 'Tex' because of his thick Texan drawl, he joined the cult after he hitched a ride with Manson and was immediately captivated by his doctrines.

Towards the end of 1968, Helter Skelter was born.

I believe that Manson had always been somewhat racist, but he began to be more open about it when he blended his views into the doctrines he was teaching. Mind-altering drugs such as acid and LSD, combined with his increasingly unstable psyche, made for a lethal combination. His teachings became darker and more radical and he convinced himself that he was receiving messages from beyond. When the Beatles released the album *The Beatles* (also known as *The White Album*), Manson convinced himself and his followers that the album contained coded messages that were directed at them. These messages supported his prophetic prediction that tensions between whites and blacks would result in an apocalyptic war, which only he and The Family would survive.

In lengthy speeches to his disciples, Manson prophesied that a civil war would take place when the whites would be divided over the way that the black population was treated, echoing a similar scenario to that which sparked the American Civil War. The conflict, which he named after the Beatles song *Helter Skelter,* would continue until the whites had ultimately killed each other off and become extinct. He claimed that the 'blackies', as he called them, would stand back while this happened, thrilled that they would be rid of the whites once and for all. But they would be unaware that members of his cult, now the only remaining whites, would be hiding in an underground city beneath Death Valley. According to his sordid tale, the black population would be incapable of ruling themselves and The Family would come out of hiding and take over as rulers.

It would be obvious to any sane person that such a tale could only be created in the mind of a deluded narcissist who was clearly under the influence of drugs. But Manson's followers, who were also constantly intoxicated, had been sucked so deep into his fantasy that they could no longer recognise the difference between reason and madness. Every word he spoke was accepted as the truth and his followers embraced his prediction without a shadow of doubt.

In November 1968, the cult moved to two abandoned ranches near Death Valley, where they could more easily make preparations for their escape into hiding. In a closed-door session in February 1969, Manson revealed his final plan. There was still no sign of the start of the civil war and therefore it was now up to them to provoke it. In order to do so, he told them that they would need to create an album that was similar to that of the Beatles, but which would contain subliminal messages for young, white females. Upon hearing it, all white women in the United States would be driven to actively search out and join The Family. According to his plan, this would lead the 'blackies' to become frustrated because of the dwindling number of white women that were available to them for sex. They would vent their anger by lashing out violently against white men, resulting in a full-scale racial war that would spark the start of Helter Skelter.

In January 1969, they moved yet again, this time because Manson had told them that they needed to be in a position to be able to monitor the conflict that was going to erupt any day now. They chose a canary yellow house, which they named after another Beatles song, 'Yellow Submarine'. There they worked on their album, practised shooting, prepared vehicles and planned their precise escape route to Death Valley. Manson was convinced there were codes to the route they should take in *The Beatles* album and they listened to it repeatedly in an attempt to decipher them.

Once the cult's album was finished, Manson made contact with his showbiz connections to try and raise some interest in the recording that he believed was destined to launch Helter Skelter. He arranged for singer and record producer, Terry Melcher, to come by their house and listen to a few of their songs. The women scrubbed the house from top to bottom and laid out a lavish meal, but Melcher failed to show up.

Furious and humiliated, Manson drove to 10050 Cielo Drive, Los Angeles, which he believed to be Melcher's place of residence. When the resident caretaker met him at the gate, he told him that Melcher was no longer living there and that he had rented the house to celebrity producer, Roman Polanski and his pregnant wife, actress Sharon Tate. Manson left the property and eventually managed to contact Melcher to arrange another visit. However, when the meeting did take place, Melcher did not show much interest in their music.

Manson's mood spiralled into a dark and bitter place. His dreams of becoming a music star were fast fading and he felt rejected by Hollywood. He turned to his bizarre fantasy once more but this time, he was ready to put his plan into action.

The first target in his quest to start Helter Skelter was Bernard Crowe, a violent drug dealer who had recently made threats towards the cult. On 1 July 1969, Crowe was shot dead in his Hollywood apartment and that same day, news outlets mistakenly identified him as belonging to the Black Panther movement. Upon hearing this, Manson and his followers panicked. Fearing retribution, they purchased additional weapons and took turns patrolling their property twenty-four hours a day. Despite this, Manson did not put the brakes on his plans. Just three weeks later, police discovered a bloody crime scene at the home of Gary Hinman, an acquaintance of the cult. The music teacher, who was known for his generosity and soft manner of speech, had been viciously stabbed and his left ear had been cut off. Behind his lifeless body, the words 'Political Piggy' had been painted on the wall with his blood and, in an attempt to divert the police's attention, the murderers also drew a paw print, which was the symbol of the Black Panther movement.

Two days earlier, Manson had sent his girlfriend, Mary Brunner, along with two of his followers, Susan Atkins and Bobby Beausoleil to Hinman's residence.

Manson believed that Hinman had recently inherited $20,000 and he wanted a portion of it for himself. But they were not prepared for Hinman to put up a fight. Refusing to hand over any money, he was held hostage for two days in his own home and had his ear cut off by Manson on one of his visits. When they realised that he would never give in, Beausoleil stabbed him to death and stole his car on his way out. It was this final act that would condemn him; just days later Beausoleil was arrested whilst driving the car with the murder weapon still in his possession. He remained loyal to Manson throughout the trial and did not implicate him, even when he was sentenced to death.

The killings had wet Manson's appetite for blood and notoriety. On 8 August 1969 he sent a team of assassins on a killing spree that would shock the world and cast a shadow of fear over the showbiz community. That warm evening, eight months' pregnant Sharon Tate bid her guests good night after a cosy dinner party. With her husband away on a business trip in London, Tate had invited three of her friends to her house to keep her company. Hairstylist Jay Sebring, aspiring screenwriter Wojciech Frykowski and his wealthy girlfriend, Abigail Folger, finished their nightcaps and also retired for the night.

In a small house at the back of the property, eighteen-year-old Steven Parent was preparing to drive home after visiting the residence's caretaker who lived there. The unsuspecting visitors and residents of the property had no idea that immense danger was lurking outside. As the clock struck midnight, cult members Tex Watson, Susan Atkins, Patricia Krenwinkel and Linda Kasabian were making their way into the property through dense bushes near the gate. Manson's instruction to Watson was very clear. He was to take three of the girls to the house and, in his words, 'totally destroy everyone in it, as gruesome as you can'. Having cut the telephone wire that was connected to the house, the cult killers crept across the lawn in complete silence, making their way towards the driveway.

But their progress was halted when they heard the sound of a car engine heading their way. The women ran back to the bushes but Watson remained on the driveway and forced the car to come to a halt. Steven Parent didn't stand a chance. With a 22-calibre gun aimed at his head, he begged for his life, but the bloodthirsty killer showed no mercy. He slashed him several times with his knife before shooting him four times. The teenager never made it off that driveway and he died alone in his car; a young life full of hopes and dreams had been extinguished for no reason. With the unexpected witness now silenced, the team moved towards the house where they found a screen window that could easily be cut through. Kasabian's role was to keep watch, and she waited outside as the other three entered the property.

Once inside the house, they woke the sleeping residents and bound them before escorting them into the living room at gunpoint. As their assailants shouted and herded them together, cries of fear and pleas for mercy rung out into the deadly silence of the night. Watson slung a rope over a ceiling beam and then grabbed heavily pregnant Tate and tied it around her neck. When her friend, Jay Sebring, protested angrily at the rough treatment that he was inflicting on her, Watson lifted his gun and shot him. Then, as the other three hostages watched in horror, he stabbed Sebring seven times to finish him off.

Meanwhile, Wojciech Frykowski had managed to wrangle himself free from his bonds and he entered into a scuffle with Atkins. She stabbed him in the legs, but he managed to escape her grip and dragged himself through the door and onto the front porch. Watson bolted after him and when he caught up, he smashed him in the head several times with his gun. So violent were his blows that he broke the gun's right grip in the process. But despite his vicious assault, Frykowski was still alive. In a last act of defiance, he began to drag himself across the front lawn, clawing at the dew soaked ground as he pulled himself forward. Sadly, his bravery was not enough to save him and Watson ended his struggle by stabbing him fifty-one times.

Back in the house, Abigail Folger had also managed to free herself and in desperation, she ran out of the house and across the pool area. Krenwinkle went after her and overpowered her when she reached the front lawn. There, despite her pleas for her life, Krenwinkle stabbed her twenty-eight times. Folger fell to the ground where she died, just a few feet away from her lover's lifeless body.

Sharon Tate's ordeal was not yet over. In the living room, she pleaded with her captors for mercy, begging them to spare the life of her child. It was to no avail. As she cried out and attempted to negotiate with them, she was stabbed sixteen times and left to die on the blood-soaked floor of her living room, with her unborn baby. The murder of any human being is despicable and evil, but the murder of a woman who is carrying a child is one of the most horrific crimes that can be committed. Using her blood, they painted the word 'pig' on the front door and fled into the night, leaving behind them the scene of a massacre.

The next morning, housekeeper Winifred Chapman arrived at the Polanski residence at 8 a.m., to begin her work for the day. As she walked up the driveway she noticed that an unfamiliar car was parked on it and that a telephone wire was draped across the front gate. When she entered the house, she froze in shock as she discovered the bodies of Sebring and Tate in the living room. Frantic, she turned and ran out the house, screaming hysterically as she stumbled across the other two bodies on the front lawn.

When police arrived at the property they were horrified. Several officers, upon seeing the mutilated bodies, were unable to control their emotions and had to be led away from the scene of the crime. The five victims had been so brutally murdered and yet there appeared to be no apparent motive or clue as to the identity of the killers. As the investigators gathered evidence, the perpetrators assembled in the front room of their house to discuss the events of the night. Manson was sorely disappointed with them, as he felt that they had not sufficiently maintained control over their victims. The crimes had been messy and disorganised; they were not the smooth executions that he had hoped for. As they enjoyed a cocktail of narcotics, he explained the level of efficiency that he expected from them on their next mission and told them that they must all play a part in future murders. Then, he announced who their next target would be.

A year earlier, Manson and several of his followers had attended a party at a house on Waverly drive, Los Angeles. Next door resided supermarket executive Leno LaBianca and his wife Rosemary. Apart from Manson's presence at the party, the couple had no connection to the cult in any way. It appears that Manson had randomly selected them as victims, putting his dark mark against them for no reason whatsoever.

Late on the night of 10 August 1969, he arrived at their residence with the four killers from the Tate murders, along with two additional disciples, Leslie Van Houten and Steve Grogan. Manson, Krenwinkle, Van Houten and Watson broke into the house and woke the couple at gunpoint. On Manson's instruction, Watson covered each of their heads with a pillowcase, which they tied down around their necks using a lamp cord. Like a proud mentor, Manson left the house, satisfied that they would carry out his instructions efficiently. Van Houten and Krenwinkle dragged Rosemary LaBianca into the kitchen, where she frantically tried to ward them off by swinging the lamp that was attached to the cord around her neck. The defenceless woman had no idea that next door, her husband was being viciously stabbed to death with a bayonet.

Watson's assault was interrupted when he heard the commotion coming from the women in the kitchen. He left the dying man long enough to visit the kitchen where he stabbed Rosemary several times, before returning to the bedroom to finish off her husband.

When he returned to the kitchen, Van Houten was repeatedly thrusting a knife into Rosemary's abdomen. Watson told her to stop and handed the knife to Krenwinkle, reminding her of Manson's instruction that they must all play a part in the killings. Rosemary's lifeless body sunk to the kitchen floor where Krenwinkle continued to puncture her with stab wounds. With their victims dead, they set about leaving their mark on the crime scene and then fled into the night.

When the couple's son arrived at the house the following morning, he made a gruesome discovery that would be forever etched into his mind. Police arrived shortly after and were stunned by the crime scene. Leno had been stabbed twelve times and the word 'war' had been carved into his chest. A steak knife had been plunged into his throat and a carving fork, into his stomach. Rosemary had been knifed forty-one times and many of the stab wounds were post-mortem. On the wall and fridge, the words 'Rise', 'Death to Pigs' and 'Helter Skelter' had been painted with blood.

Incredibly, it was later discovered that the LaBianca couple were not the only victims that had been targeted that night. The remainder of the team that had left the house with Manson had been dropped off at another address to carry out a second murder spree. But Kasabian intentionally knocked on the wrong door and they were forced to abandon their plan.

The police were baffled by this string of murders for which there was no apparent motive. The investigations into both serial killings were carried out separately, as certain members of the police department believed the LaBianca murders were the work of a copycat killer. It was not until November that they had a breakthrough in the case. Susan Atkins was awaiting trial for an unrelated murder when she openly confessed to her cellmate that she was involved in the Tate murders. The story exploded from there and police learnt of the dark and conniving man who appeared to be at the helm of this hippy gang of killers – Charles Manson. Atkins claimed that there were other celebrities on their list of 'pigs' that needed to die and she went into great detail to describe her deadly plans for each of them. She wanted to skin Frank Sinatra alive, tear apart Elizabeth Taylor's face by carving 'Helter Skelter' across it, and rape Tom Jones before slitting his throat. These admissions caused extreme panic among celebrities in Hollywood, and across the globe. Fearing that they may be on the cult's hit list, numerous stars fled Los Angeles and spent millions of dollars on bodyguards and security equipment.

Sordid details of the cult's lifestyle and beliefs began to emerge and arrests were made as, one by one, the names of the killers were revealed. Kasabian handed herself in voluntarily when she heard that there was a warrant out for her arrest. She claimed she had no direct involvement in the killings and even told police officers she had tried to stop the Tate massacre by telling the others that there was someone approaching the gate to the property. Because of this, she was granted immunity in exchange for her testimony.

The first trial began on 15 June 1970. Manson, Atkins, Van Houten and Krenwinkle stood accused for their involvement in the Tate and LaBianca murders. It was an explosive trial that dominated the news for the majority of its nine-month duration, notably when the bizarre Helter Skelter tale was revealed. Cult members stalked the courtroom causing disruptions and carrying out strange demonstrations, such as crawling down busy sidewalks on their hands and knees to express their undying dedication to Manson. When their leader shaved his head and carved an 'x' into his forehead, the three girls did likewise.

Witnesses for the prosecution were sent death threats and subjected to assaults in an attempt to intimidate them into backing down. One witness was badly burnt in a mysterious fire in his van, while another had her food spiked and nearly overdosed on the LSD it contained. Manson had no intention of going down quietly either; he tried to attack the judge, Charles Older, when the latter denied his request to cross-examine a prosecution witness. It was rumoured that the judge began carrying a gun under his robe from that point on.

On 16 November, the prosecution rested its case and, surprisingly, just three days later the defence also rested their case without calling a single witness. Atkins, Van Houten and Krenwinkle were outraged and demanded to be given the right to testify. In chambers, the defence lawyers explained their reasoning to the judge. They knew that their clients only wanted to take the stand in order to testify that Manson had no involvement in the crimes and, in their opinion, they would not be acting in their client's best interest if they allowed this to happen. Van Houten's lawyer, Ronald Hugues, was the most vocal of the three lawyers. He told the judge that he suspected his client was being coerced to testify by Manson, who was looking to save himself.

Ronald Hugues vanished shortly after and closing arguments had to be made by a replacement lawyer. In January 1971, the four accused were given guilty verdicts. On the day of their sentencing, Ronald Hugues' body was found wedged between boulders in a gorge. Cause of death could not be determined due to the level of decomposition and his killer was never brought to justice. However a member of the Manson Family later claimed that he had been assassinated by a member of the cult. Manson and his three followers were sent to death row, but their sentences were changed to life imprisonment when the death penalty was temporarily eliminated. Watson was tried separately as he had to be extradited from Texas. In October 1971, he too was sentenced to death, despite his lawyer's attempt to portray him as mentally ill.

In the months that followed, further murders were linked to the cult. Donald Shea, a horse wrangler who worked on the Spahn ranch, had been killed in August of 1969. Manson was one of three cult members that were found guilty of his murder, although it is not clear why he was killed. Perhaps he discovered something about the cult and needed to be silenced. Rumours also suggested that he may have been targeted because he was married to an African American woman.

In subsequent trials, Atkins, Grogan and Manson were charged and found guilty for their involvement in the Gary Hinman murder. Manson was also found guilty for the murder of drug dealer Bernard Crowe. His girlfriend, Mary

Brunner, having not participated directly in the murders, was offered immunity for her testimony. The evil cult leader remains in prison to this day as inmate B33920 at Corcoran State Prison in Kings County, California. On 11 April 2012, he was denied parole for the twelfth time and he is not permitted to reapply for another fifteen years, at which time he will be ninety-two years of age. But, even then, it is very unlikely that he will be released. He will always remain a danger to society because of his ability to manipulate and control minds to such an extent that they willingly commit atrocious crimes for him. That type of power does not fade with age. As long as there are naïve minds in the world which are open to such manipulation, he remains a threat.

In 1987, MSNBC carried out an interview with Manson, which was considered so appalling, that it was only aired in its entirety in 2007 on the TV programme *Mind of Manson*. The producers found the footage of 'unshackled, unapologetic and unruly' Manson so unbelievable that they only allowed seven minutes of it to be aired when it was first released.

I watched the interview and was surprised at how openly aggressive and menacing Manson was towards his female interviewer. He is rude, obnoxious and demonstrates a severe superiority complex. He rambles on, at times not making any sense, perhaps in an attempt to come across as insane. But he fails miserably as, in other parts of the interview, he portrays his intelligent and manipulative side, taking full control of the interview as if he was the interviewer.

At one point in the interview he complains about the way he has been treated in jail. He glares at the interviewer as he says, 'if you spit in my face and smack me in the mouth and throw me into solitary confinement for nothing, what do you think is going to happen to you when I get out of here?' As he finishes his sentence, he turns away from the interviewer and stares straight into the camera lens. His dark eyes bore through the screen, delivering a threat to each viewer personally. A chill ran down my spine.

He has absolutely no remorse and instead tries to pin the blame for his crimes on other people, or deflect the attention onto world issues, such as the destruction the human race has caused to our planet earth. He even tries to joke: '...believe me, if I started murdering people there would be none of you left'. It is a threat that hopefully sways the parole board each time his application comes up.

Sadly, Manson will never be forgotten. But it is his victims that we should remember rather than him. There may be other bodies out there that were never discovered, but we can be certain of twelve victims: Bernard Crowe, Gary Hinman, Steven Parent, Sharon Tate, her unborn child Paul Richard Polanski, Jay Sebring, Wojciech Frykowski, Abigail Folger, Leno and Rosemary LaBianca, Ronald Hugues and Donald Shea.

CHAPTER 7

The People's Temple: Jim Jones

So my opinion is that you be kind to children and be kind to seniors and take the potion like they used to take in ancient Greece and step over quietly because we are not committing suicide; it's a revolutionary act. [...] Die with a degree of dignity. Lay down your life with dignity. Don't lay down with tears and agony. There's nothing to death, it's just stepping over to another plane [...] Look children, it's just something to put you to rest. Oh, God. Mother, Mother, Mother, Mother, Mother, please. Mother, please, please, please. Don't—don't do this. Don't do this. Lay down your life with your child. But don't do this. Keep—keep your emotions down. Keep your emotions down. Children, it will not hurt. If you'd be—if you'll be quiet. If you'll be quiet. [...] Let's be dignified. If you quit tell them they're dying—if you adults would stop some of this nonsense. Adults, adults, adults. I call on you to stop this nonsense. I call on you to quit exciting your children when all they're doing is going to a quiet rest. I call on you to stop this now if you have any respect at all. Are we black, proud, and Socialist, or what are we? Now stop this nonsense. Don't carry this on anymore. You're exciting your children [...] Take our life from us. We laid it down. We got tired. We didn't commit suicide, we committed an act of revolutionary suicide protesting the conditions of an inhumane world.

Throughout his final speech on 18 November 1978, Jim Jones's voice is slurred and, at times, he is incoherent. In the background you can hear the cries and screams of young children and babies who are being coaxed to swallow a cyanide poison mix, which is being fed to them forcefully through a large syringe. As the children's cries grow quieter, the adults' wailing grows louder as they watch their offspring draw their last breaths. What sort of a man is capable of convincing so many people to commit such a large-scale murder-suicide? What sort of parent kills their own child?

Born in Indiana on 13 May 1931, Jim Jones was an only child in a poor family who struggled to make ends meet. His father was a First World War veteran who was disabled following a mustard gas accident. He was also an alcoholic, and rumoured to have had ties with the Ku Klux Klan. His mother was the sole breadwinner and was often absent, leaving Jones alone for long periods.

According to his childhood friends, he was an odd child who had an obsession with religion and death. One told of how he once killed a cat and then organised a mock funeral for it, which he invited his friends to attend. He was also regularly seen shouting out sermons from his front porch, hoping that people passing on the street would stop and listen. But, as with many cult leaders, he was also very intelligent and he excelled in school, passing his high school degree early and with honours in 1948. He went to university and married Marceline Baldwin in 1949.

He was initially inspired by communism, but pretty soon he realised that the church was where his greed for money and power would be filled. Hence, after trying out several churches and receiving training, he opened his own fellowship, The People's Temple.

Having been an outcast in his childhood, Jones felt that he could relate to the black community in Indiana and he used that to expand his church. He adopted a 'revival pastor' persona and his sermons were loud and flamboyant, much like those that took place in gospel churches. He brought new followers through the doors using messages about interracial peace and powerful demonstrations of healing. It would later be discovered that all his miracles were fake. Chicken organs were placed on a tray and paraded through his congregation as proof that a tumour had been removed from one of his followers. Jones' close friends would disguise themselves as invalids and attend his sermons so that they could be publically 'healed' by him.

At the start it appeared to be very much an enthusiastic evangelical church whose main focus was helping the poor, homeless and the elderly whilst promoting racial integration. To further prove his doctrine, he adopted children of various races which he called his 'rainbow family'; three Asian American children, an African American and a Native American child formed his multi-coloured family. He later adopted two Caucasian children and had a biological child with his wife, Marceline.

In his years in Indiana, he had dabbled in political roles. Appointed Director of the Human Rights Commission by the Mayor of Indianapolis in 1960, he ignored the advice he was given to remain low key and instead used his position to broadcast his political opinions and religious messages through media outlets. He gave many interviews and it is rumoured that he was behind a scandalous incident involving the painting of swastikas on the outside walls of two residences where African American families lived. The swastika has been considered a symbol of racism since the Nazis used it as the infamous marking on their flag. Understandably, the families who resided at both residences were horrified and Jones arranged to visit them after the event to demonstrate his support, all under the watchful eye of the media. He protested against the separation of blacks and whites in hospital wards, which caused health officials to change their wards to a mixed set up.

These actions did not go unnoticed and his fame grew steadily in the years that followed. By the early sixties he had over 300 followers in his church. During this time, he also embarked on a trip with his wife and children as he had become convinced that a nuclear apocalypse would take place. After reading in a magazine that Belo Horizonte in Brazil would be a safe location in the event of a nuclear war, he brought his family there to set up a new church, passing through Guyana *en route*. The following year, unsatisfied with the lack of opportunity in Belo Horizonte, they moved to Rio de Janeiro where they remained for several months, carrying out charity work and attempting to recruit followers.

But Jones could not stay away for long. He was worried that his position back home would be threatened in his absence and his suspicions were confirmed when his leadership team sent him a report listing issues that were occurring within the church. He returned to Indiana immediately and, not long after, he made an announcement to his followers. He told them that the nuclear apocalypse would occur on 15 July 1967, but reassured them that they would be safe if they followed him to California, where they would wait until it was all over and then help him create a new socialist government that would rule the earth.

In 1965, Jones and his family, along with seventy of his closest followers, moved to northern California in search of a place where they would be safe in the event of a nuclear war. They found their haven in Redwood Valley near Ukiah, where they set up a community.

From there, the movement spread to San Francisco and Los Angeles as Jones embarked on tours to spread his doctrine. Travelling with a fleet of old silver buses, he stopped at various venues to influence congregations with his charismatic speeches and healing sessions. His doctrines were, at this stage, already growing further apart from the foundations of Christianity. He began to criticise the Bible and to question the existence of God, going so far as to suggest that he himself was God.

What you need to believe in is what you can see... If you see me as your friend, I'll be your friend. If you see me as your father, I'll be your father, for those of you that don't have a father... If you see me as your saviour, I'll be your saviour. If you see me as your God, I'll be your God.

He also invented the bizarre doctrine that he was the only true heterosexual on earth and that all others were bi-sexual. He condemned sex as a distraction and yet he himself was indulging in sexual relations with both women and men within his church when it suited him.

In 1974, he sent a small team of his most dedicated disciples to Guyana to begin clearing the tropical forest near the Venezuelan border for an agricultural settlement. Nearly 4,000 acres of wild jungle territory had been leased by Jones from the Government of Guyana for a period of twenty-five years. Far from surrounding villages and completely isolated from outside influence, they began to carve a town into the dense growth, which they believed would become their safe haven. They called it the 'People's Temple Agricultural Project'.

By 1975, his congregation had expanded to over 7,000 members of various backgrounds, races and social standing. With such large numbers, the church was blossoming financially. Devoted followers sold their houses and gave all their belongings and savings to the church, predominantly elderly members, who were promised by Jones that they would be looked after for the rest of their lives. He opened care homes for the elderly, which enabled him to attract even more of these vulnerable souls. Younger members worked regular jobs and handed in their wages to the church, receiving a small allowance in return and dedicating the remainder of their time to working on church projects, even if this meant sleeping only a couple of hours a night.

Jones decided to move his headquarters to San Francisco in the hope of advancing his political career. He began using the large numbers of followers that he had to further his political power, by secretly renting out his congregation to local politicians to boost their numbers at political rallies and during elections. With the assistance of the church, politician George Moscone won the mayoral election, after which Jones was appointed as Chairman of the San Francisco Housing Authority Commission. He gained the support of many local and national political figures such as vice presidential candidate Walter Mondale, who publically praised the church, and first Lady Rosalynn Carter who personally met with him on several occasions. He was even awarded the Glide's Martin Luther King Jr Humanitarian Award in recognition for his work in local communities.

But, as often occurs, large-scale publicity attracted not only supporters but the attention of journalists, who were looking for a story. As Jones's public image grew, *Chronicle* reporter, Marshall Kilduff, began to take a keen interest in the People's Temple and in Jim Jones in particular. He began to search for defectors who could tell him more about life as a member of this radical church. Initially, he found it difficult to find people who were willing to speak but, eventually, he was put in contact with an ex-member who wanted to expose Jones, and before long others followed.

Kilduff was horrified when he heard their stories. The public image that the People's Temple portrayed to the world was one that was carefully orchestrated to appear as a united, loving church whose members had dedicated their lives to equality and helping people in need. The reality, however, was a far cry from that image.

Behind the double-bolted doors of their community, members were forced to attend sermons most nights of the week, at times running through until dawn. In these nightly events, followers would be publically humiliated and disgraced during catharsis sessions, in which a member would be singled out and criticised by the others in the room. These sessions had turned violent in recent years with public beatings and boxing matches arranged to punish members who Jones felt were not performing at their best, or who had refused to turn over their money. Children were not exempt and were regularly beaten for insignificant sins. Kilduff was also told about the 'healing' performances and the true extent of the financial wealth that Jones had accumulated from his followers over the years. Some claimed they had been sexually abused by higher placed members or by Jones himself.

Kilduff and his colleague, Phil Tracy, put together a hard-hitting article exposing the People's Temple and calling for an investigation to be carried out. Kilduff approached his employer at the *Chronicle* and asked if they wanted to run the story. He was met with resistance, which was hardly surprising considering Jones had connections in the media and had previously made a donation to a charity that the *Chronicle* championed. However, Kilduff was not about to give up and he approached *New West Magazine*, who jumped at the opportunity to publish his scandalous story.

Somehow, Jones got wind of the upcoming article and he even managed to obtain a copy of it in advance. Knowing that he had little chance to save his reputation, he packed up and fled to Guyana just before the magazine was published. He sent word to the thousands of followers he left behind, inviting them to join him. Along with his invitation, he sent a propaganda film of their agricultural town that portrayed happy pioneer families and a simple, yet beautiful village that was filled with enough food and housing for all. Over 2,000 applied for a place in his jungle community and around 1,000 were accepted. Before long, a steady stream of expats arrived by land, air and sea and the once scarcely populated town was brimming with habitants. Jones nicknamed the village Jonestown, after himself.

Jones's mind was in a very dark state when he arrived in Guyana. He had started taking drugs a couple of years prior and was increasingly paranoid and on edge. He began raving to his followers that the US government was trying to assassinate him and that they would come after the whole group and kill them.

In one particular church session, he carried out a cruel test of loyalty on his members. When they had first arrived at the church, he had offered them all a glass of punch as refreshment. But, some time into his sermon, once they had all finished their drinks, he announced the punch had been poisoned. The room erupted into a storm of hysteria as members fell into each other's arms crying and bidding their loved ones farewell. He allowed their despair to continue for a few minutes until he told them it was not true, but that it had been a test for what may have to come in the future. He then told them about 'translation', his theory that they would all die together and move to another planet where they would live in pure happiness forever.

Following this incident, a divide began to form amongst his flock. Many began to doubt Jones's sanity, while even those who still believed in him felt that he had let them down. Life in Jonestown was not as he had promised and some felt betrayed and unsatisfied. The community was almost self-sufficient but they still required funds in order to live. To raise income, they grew crops such as pineapple, cassava, eddoes, and other tropical fruits and vegetables. They also raised livestock for consumption and produced basic toys and items to sell.

Members were expected to work long hours each day and endure lengthy sermons each evening. Even when they returned to their cramped, poorly furnished living quarters, they still had to listen to the loud ramblings that emerged from a speaker system that was connected to all areas of the compound. Jones had sermons blaring out twenty-four hours a day, some pre-recorded and others live. He fed them worldwide 'news updates', which were all incorrect or heavily distorted and designed to instil a deep fear of leaving the compound. In one speech, he announced that the United States and the United Kingdom had decided to deport all residents that were of Asian or African descent. Being that the majority of his community was African-American, he was making it clear to them that they had no home to return to, and therefore, would be better off staying in Jonestown for life.

When they were in the fields slaving away, they could hear him. When they were lying in bed, they could hear him. When they woke up, his voice was the first they heard. Every moment of every day, his doctrines were pounded into them like a drug; a drug making them weak, submissive, loyal and focused solely on him. But some members had another type of drug on their mind.

Ever since they had lived in close proximity with their leader, it became harder and harder not to notice his drug addiction. Even through the speakers, his voice was increasingly slurred and his ramblings incoherent.

As time went on, several of his followers also began to realise that they were no longer free to come and go as they pleased. Armed guards patrolled the outskirts of the town, security posts were set up and tighter restrictions on movement were put into place. Some of his more alert members realised that they had become prisoners, while others were blissfully ignorant, still blinded by their loyalty to Jones and their firm belief that he was protecting them from an outside enemy.

Drills were organised, during which Jones would secretly order one member of a family to attempt an escape and then wait to see if their relatives reported their crime to him. Children turned on their parents, husbands and wives gave each other up, brothers and sisters betrayed one another. Jones had them exactly where he wanted them; they were so loyal to him that nothing else mattered. Those who tried to rebel were put into isolation and, when they were let out, appeared to be in a dazed, drugged state with no willpower left to fight back.

Meanwhile, in the US, family and friends of members living in Jonestown were frantic. They united to form a group called 'Concerned Relatives' and organised protests in the streets, claiming their loved ones were being held against their will. They begged authorities for help to get them back and distributed leaflets outside government offices to attract the public's attention.

Although Jones had lost many of his supporters in the political world, he still had friends who defended him. Politicians George Moscone, Willie Brown and Harvey Milk all stood by Jones, claiming that he had not broken any laws.

The Concerned Relatives were not about to give up and they upped their campaign to free their loved ones. Tim Stoen was a key member and one of the founders of the organisation. He and his wife, Grace, were ex-members of the People's Temple and it was rumoured that Jones fathered their son, John Stoen. When Grace left the cult, she began a custody battle to retrieve her son. Jones advised Tim to bring his son to Jonestown so that he would not have to give him up. He did just that but, when he himself defected in June 1977, he was forced to leave his son behind. Once back on US soil, he and his wife began a legal battle to force Jones to return their child.

Determined, Stoen travelled to Washington in January 1978 and appealed to Congressmen and State Department officials, including Congressman Leo Ryan, who upon hearing his story, became immediately concerned about the situation. Being a hands-on politician, he decided he had to travel to Jonestown on a fact-finding mission to see for himself if members were being held against their will.

By November, they were ready to begin their trip. Ryan travelled with his entourage, a group of media reporters and several members of Relatives Concerned, including Tim and Grace Stoen. In the hope that Ryan would retrieve their son, the Stoens decided to stay at a hotel in neighbouring Georgetown as they knew that as defectors, it would be too dangerous for them to visit Jonestown.

The group arrived in Georgetown on 15 November and, two days later, Ryan and his staff, along with the journalists, travelled onwards to Jonestown. When they arrived at the entrance of the town, they were greeted by rows of smiling cult members who welcomed them with handmade banners and cheers. Things were off to a good start and Ryan was hopeful that this trip would put to rest any concerns about the cult.

While they were given a tour of the grounds and introduced to its habitants, Ryan began to wonder if the rumours were, in fact, vicious lies that had been spun by bitter ex-members. He was rather impressed with what he was seeing. He found the town to be self-sufficient, well run and friendly. That evening, they organised a reception for him where there was music and dancing and Ryan was increasingly sure that he had been misled. He rose and gave a short speech to the large sea of cult members in the pavilion, telling them that he was very happy with what he had seen so far. The crowd went wild, cheering and clapping for a few minutes before carrying on with the party. But, in the back of the room, a couple of Jones's disciples were desperate enough to risk their lives in an attempt to escape.

Amidst the noise and hubbub of the party, Jonestown habitant Vernon Gosney slipped a note to journalist Don Harris, believing he was Congressman Ryan.

'Dear Congressman, Vernon Gosney and Monica Bagby. Please help us get out of Jonestown.'

Harris discreetly informed Ryan of the note, but they took no immediate action. As the evening progressed, Ryan watched Jones intently, and it dawned on him that he had been fooled by a sinister con artist. Paying close attention, he noticed the way that Jones's every glance held his followers in submission; there was fear behind the fake merriness of the party. Ryan met with his team later that night in private, to discuss what action they needed to take.

Early the next morning, 18 November 1978, eleven habitants of Jonestown managed to sneak past the guards and flee into the jungle. They sensed that the situation was becoming very dangerous and would later realise just how right they were.

Ryan and his team were taken on a tour of the town that morning and, by the time they returned, dark clouds were rolling in as a rainstorm approached. At this point, Ryan cleverly used Jones's own words to his advantage, telling him that if, as he claimed, he was not holding his followers against their will, then he should prove it by allowing those who wanted to leave the premises to join him and his team when they returned home. Jones reluctantly agreed.

By early afternoon, two families had requested to leave with Ryan. Jones granted his permission, as he did for Gosney and Bagby, the authors of the note. When Harris confronted Jones with the note, the cult leader brushed it aside, claiming defectors were all liars and were out to destroy Jonestown. As he spoke, another father and his children approached him, requesting to leave. Furious, Jones could no longer maintain his false image of calm and he began to argue with Ryan. By this point, the storm outside was in full swing; the sky was black as coal and the heavy rain crashed to the ground like a torrent of bullets. Clusters of cult members surrounded the tense exchange between Jones and Ryan's team, crying and wailing out of fear and distress at what was taking place. Ryan knew that this emotionally charged situation could only get worse. He instructed his team to accompany those leaving to the airstrip, whilst he and Richard Dwyer, Deputy Chief of the US Embassy in Guyana, stayed behind to wait for any last-minute leavers.

Just as the dump truck was leaving, cult member Larry Layton jumped aboard, demanding to be allowed to leave as well. Other defectors found this suspicious, as Larry was known to be a dedicated, almost fanatical member of the church; however, they allowed him to join them, thinking he may have had a change of heart.

Shortly after they left, Ryan was attacked by cult member Don Sly who launched himself at him with a knife and had to be wrestled to the ground by other Temple members. The congressman was left shaken but unharmed. He told his team that they had to leave immediately, and they made their way to the airstrip with the others.

When they arrived, most of the group had already boarded the first plane and Ryan's team prepared to board a second, smaller aircraft. As the larger plane began to taxi down the airstrip, Larry Layton pulled out a gun and began firing at the other passengers on board, wounding Gosney and Bagby. He was disarmed by fellow passengers as their aircraft ground to a halt at the end of the runway. Meanwhile, at the other end of the dirt airstrip, Ryan and his team were boarding their aircraft when they noticed that a tractor was heading for them at full speed, dragging a trailer behind it. As it reached the airstrip, eight men jumped out of the trailer, lifted their guns and began firing shots at them. Congressman Ryan, photographer Greg Robinson, NBC reporter Don Harris and Temple defector Patricia Parks were all killed in the first few minutes of the shooting. Cameraman Bob Brown managed to film a few seconds of the attack before he too, was mowed down by the cold-hearted assassins. Deputy Chief Dwyer and eight others lay critically injured in the red dirt of the airstrip as the gunmen fled.

Back in Jonestown, Jim Jones had reached the point of no return. He told his attorney, Charles Garry, that all was lost. Garry attempted to placate him by reminding him that Ryan had promised to write a positive report about their community; clearly, the attorney was not aware of the attack that Jones had ordered on the airstrip. Had he been, he would have known that matters had escalated beyond repair.

Jones gathered his followers in the pavilion and began a forty-four minute death speech which he recorded. He told them what his men had done at the airstrip and warned them that the US government would want revenge and would be sending an army to slaughter them all. He urged his people to commit revolutionary suicide and was challenged by only one of his followers. Christine Miller suggested that there was an alternative, reminding Jones of their back-up plan to move to Russia. Jones, slurring and mumbling his words, argued back, insisting it was too late to form a plan to airlift everyone there. Miller persisted, telling him that the children deserved to live and voicing her view that to die was an acceptance of defeat. He became cross with her and other members joined in, insisting that she back down which she eventually did.

Midway through his speech, his assassins returned and Jones announced to his congregation that Ryan had been killed and urged them to begin their mass suicide. The first victim, a mother and her one-year-old infant, approached the large container that contained the poison. For the children, who were put to death first, a large syringe was used to force feed them a dose of the lethal drink. It was a concoction of cyanide, grape-flavoured juice and sedatives that killed them within five minutes.

The remainder of the recording is tragic, heart wrenching and surreal. Jones is heard egging his people on as he circulates the room to make sure that they are heading towards the drink stand. Understandably some of the adults, having witnessed the children dying, demonstrate hesitation. Several of his followers can be heard taking the microphone to give speeches about how much they love their leader and are grateful that he is their father. The cries and screams of the children in the background continues throughout the first part of the recording, but then begins to die down as the last of the youngsters slips into death and the remaining adults step up to the stand. After each one takes their dose, they are led outside where they are made to lie down on the muddy earth, and left to die.

Jones can be heard losing patience towards the end as he begs his followers to hurry up and get it over with. Sensing that they are hesitating, he continues to encourage them with promises of a joyous afterlife, while his armed guards circle the outside of the pavilion to prevent people from leaving. The sound of weeping continues in the background as Jones carries on.

I tell you, I don't care how many screams you hear, I don't care how many anguished cries... death is a million times preferable to ten more days of this life. If you knew what was ahead of you—if you knew what was ahead of you, you'd be glad to be stepping over tonight.

In the last minute of the tape, Jones is still mumbling but the background noise grows eerily quiet... a deadly silence that speaks for itself.

Jones shot himself in the head. He had encouraged his people to die a painful death by poisoning and yet was too cowardly to take the poison himself. He took the easy way out and shot himself in the left temple. When the tragedy was discovered, it shocked the entire world.

Rows of bodies covered the ground surrounding the pavilion, and other areas of the town. Some 909 people died that day in Jonestown, 304 of which were children, including John Stoen, who was found dead in Jones's cabin. Most died of poisoning, though a few were found with gunshot wounds. Many appeared to have been forced to take the poison as needle marks were later discovered on bodies, which suggested that they were injected, most likely because they refused to drink the mixture.

A few survived and escaped Jonestown. The defectors who were on the airstrip all made it out alive, including Larry Layton, the shooter who infiltrated the group when they were leaving. He was later tried for attempted murder in Guyana, but was let off as he was found to have been significantly brain washed. In the US, they could not try him for attempted murder on Guyanese soil, but they tried him for conspiracy and aiding and abetting the murder of a member of Congress, Leo Ryan, and for the attempted murder of an internationally protected individual, Richard Dwyer. He was released on parole in 2002.

It was the greatest single loss of American civilian life in a non-natural disaster prior to 11 September 2001. And it was still not over.

At the cult's office in Georgetown, Sharon Amos received a radio communication from Jonestown as the murder-suicides were commencing. They instructed her to take revenge on the Temple's enemies and then to commit revolutionary suicide. Later that evening, when police arrived at her door to question her, she led her three children to the bathroom; using a kitchen knife, she stabbed her ten- and eleven-year-old children first, and then instructed her teenage daughter to stab her, before taking her own life.

With five murders at the airstrip and four in Georgetown, the total number of lives that perished at the hands of this twisted cult leader was 918.

The Guyanese and US military had the gruesome task of cleaning up Jonestown and ensuring each body was correctly identified and returned home to their grieving relatives. The town remained closed for a few years and then was used as a refugee camp for a short period, before being abandoned again. A fire later destroyed the majority of the town and the rest is now being reclaimed by the forest.

Despite there being many shocking images available that portray the horrific mass graveyard that Jonestown became, I chose not to include these in my book out of respect for the victims. In particular the children, who could not have made the decision to commit suicide and, hence, were victims of murder.

In the years that followed the tragedy, many rumours and wild speculations circulated the media. Some claimed that Jones was not dead, but living in hiding with a few of his closest followers. There were also rumours that the deaths were not suicides but a prearranged assassination carried out by the CIA. These theories are completely unfounded and from witness accounts it is clear that the deaths were simply caused by one deranged man who, although he may have started out with good intentions, in the end could not resist the lure of power and money that religion brought him. So many people died because of one man's deluded mind that had been further twisted by drugs. Jonestown is an extreme example of just how powerful one person can be in a cult environment. It is an incident that society must learn from and prevent from ever happening again.

CHAPTER 8

The Witch Doctor:
Adolfo Constanzo

Adolfo de Jesus Constanzo was born on 1 November 1962 in Miami, Florida, to a fifteen-year-old Cuban immigrant and occult priestess, Delia Gonzalez. His parents fervently practised a religion called Palo Mayombe, which originated from the Congo. It holds values of both good and evil equally, with no discrimination between the two. Its followers have the choice to choose a good or evil god to serve, which makes it a popular religion for many criminals.

The practice includes rituals with altars to venerate the spirits of ancestors and the powers of the earth and nature. It also involves various spells for good fortune, money or anything else that the requestor's heart desires. Potions are used which include strange ingredients, such as water that has been boiled with human bones and the blood and body parts of animals.

Constanzo's young parents believed that their son was special and had a great destiny ahead of him. They had him blessed by a Haitian priest at six months of age and pampered him endlessly. When his father passed away, Gonzalez took her baby son with her to Puerto Rico, where she remarried. To please her new husband, she had Constanzo baptised in a Catholic Church; however, when he was not around, she secretly practised her own occult religion and ensured that she instilled in her son the same loyalty to their faith. She arranged secret outings, taking Constanzo with her to religious lectures and rituals so that he could learn their doctrines. Gonzalez truly believed that her son would become the greatest Palo Mayombe priest that ever existed and she had every intention of grooming him as such.

However, in 1972, Gonzalez's second husband also died and they returned to Miami where she married again, but this time to a man who was a Palo Mayombe follower and a drug dealer.

By the time Constanzo was a teenager, his mother had had three children, all from different fathers. Despite her maternal responsibilities, she was regularly arrested for shoplifting and other petty crimes, but she was never charged—a fact, which she told her son, was down to the protection of their dark religion. Often, she would terrorise her neighbours, leaving beheaded animals on their doorsteps if they angered her in any way. Rumour that she was a witch spread around the neighbourhood and the whole family became highly unpopular.

Constanzo soon followed in his mother's footsteps, with regular visits to the local police station for minor theft and vandalism. From the age of ten he spent a large portion of his time with an old Haitian Palo Mayombe priest, who introduced him to a world of satanic witchcraft and drug dealing. The priest taught Constanzo pagan religious practices as his apprentice, regularly beating him to desensitise him to pain and violence. With terrible grades at school, he seemed to have no other option in life but follow the path of witchcraft. He was so fascinated by Satanism and the dark arts that it did not take long for him to become deeply immersed. He assisted the priest with robbing body parts from graveyards and participated in his perverse rituals.

As a teenager, he went public with his bisexuality and spent most of his evenings in gay bars, where he stole from intoxicated customers. But, despite his criminal behaviour, his mother was still just as firm in her belief that he was born to fulfil a great destiny. This faith in her son only increased when, in 1981, an event that he had allegedly foretold took place. Gonzalez claimed that, five years earlier, her son had predicted the assassination attempt on US President Ronald Reagan—which, indeed, came true. There was no doubt in her mind that her cherished son would go on to great things, which he did, but in a terrible way.

At the age of twenty-one, Constanzo visited Mexico City, where he met and seduced two young men, Martin Quintana and Omar Orea. They became his first disciples and, when he relocated to Mexico City the following year, they moved in with him and took on the roles of his submissive lovers who waited on his every need and desire.

When he first relocated he earned his living as a tarot card reader while he built up his business as a satanic witch. Shortly before he left Miami, he had chosen his path and pledged himself to the dark lord, Kadiempembe, in a mystic ceremony with his priest. His mentor carved initiation symbols into his flesh with a ritual knife and gave him a *nganga*, an iron cauldron that was used to cast spells and create potions. He also formed an allegiance with the pagan god Eshu, who is known for his trickster behaviour and ability to confuse and manipulate people as he wishes. A devious and malicious god, he is able to transform his own image and take on any persona, manner of speech and appearance in order to fool those that he preys upon. These were skills that Constanzo would regularly use in the years to come and, now that he was fully qualified as a dark witch, he had every intention of abusing his power.

He began to build up a group of clients to whom he offered various services, such as protective charms, cleansing rituals and psychic readings. Very quickly his client list boomed as he became reputed as an effective witch who produced results. Police officials, drug lords and mafia godfathers were among his impressive clientele, who used his services in secret and were willing to pay up to $5,000 for a single spell.

With his success came great wealth and, after barely two years in Mexico, he had purchased a luxurious penthouse and several deluxe vehicles. Although he had a large group of clients, only a small portion of them belonged to his exclusive inner circle. Approximately forty were members of his cult and were allowed to take part in his macabre satanic rituals, which included the use of human body parts to create potions in his cauldron. Most were obtained from cemeteries across the city; but, in 1987, he and several cult members murdered a family of seven after a disagreement with them. When police found their bodies, they were horrified to find that several of their organs and other body parts had been removed including a spine, hearts, ears, brains and reproductive organs.

With no leads or witnesses, the murder case went cold. However, Constanzo still felt under pressure and he decided to move his cult to the isolated Santa Elena Ranch, just outside Matamoros near the US border. With nothing to hold him back, he threw himself into his rituals and became deeply involved in international drug trafficking. His disciples nicknamed him El Padrino de Matamoros, meaning the Godfather of Matamoros, and were increasingly under his mysterious spell.

The level of witchcraft he offered his clients went up a notch and, in exchange for large sums of money, he promised his powerful crime bosses protection from authorities and great wealth from their illegal operations. It later turned out that this 'protection' involved bribing police officers to turn a blind eye to the felonies that his customers were carrying out. If a rival threatened one of his client's businesses, they would mysteriously disappear, which only embellished his reputation as an impressive witch and psychic. To satisfy his never-ending need for body parts, Constanzo and his close followers shot and mutilated not only rival drug dealers, but innocent civilians who had the misfortune to cross their path.

Despite living in a world of drugs, the cult leader never used any narcotics himself, nor did he allow his disciples to use them. When one cult member, Jorge Valente, broke this rule, Constanzo had no mercy; he slaughtered him and used his body to feed his cauldron.

Over the following year, dozens of men were killed. The depraved witch became crueller and more sadistic with every kill, imposing excruciatingly painful deaths on his victims by torturing them for hours before he ended their lives. As he sank deeper into his dark and evil world, he began to perform the killings as a part of his rituals, raping and often cutting his victims while they were still alive as he insisted that they must die screaming in order for the black magic to be effective. He believed that the evil spirits he served fed on the pain of his human sacrifices and that his power would grow if he pleased them.

However, he would make a big mistake in early 1989 when he ordered his men to find him an American for his next ritual. They had already killed one man for this very ritual, but Constanzo did not feel that he had died in sufficient pain for his body parts to be used in the spell he had been commissioned to cast, which was to protect a shipment of drugs that was being transported into the US.

Matamoros was rife with American students at this time of year. Being at such a close proximity to the US border, it attracted great numbers of college students, who would travel there on breaks to party and enjoy the many prostitutes and strip clubs of the town. The young men visiting the town that spring break were blissfully unaware that each one of them was a potential target for a group of devil-worshipping killers.

Mark Kilroy, a twenty-one-year-old pre-med student from Texas, would pay a heavy price for his presence in the border town that spring. In the early hours of 14 March 1989, he disappeared during a night out with friends. Unfortunately for Constanzo, Kilroy was not a man who could vanish without alarms being raised. When his friends reported him missing and contacted his well-connected relatives, the story made news headlines in the US within days and Mexican authorities were put under immense pressure to find out what had happened to the young man.

Under the watchful eye of US foreign officials, police in Matamoros arrested every known criminal in the area and interrogated them, using brutality when required to press the case forward. Nearly 150 ex-cons were questioned, but nothing came of it. Kilroy's relatives upped the ante, offering a $15,000 reward for his safe return. They could not have known that the bright young lad had been lured away from his friends that night and bludgeoned to death with a shower of machete blows to the back of his skull.

As the search went on, a completely unrelated police initiative was also taking place along the Mexican side of the US border. Roadblocks had been set up and police cars patrolled the border carrying out random searches of passing cars, looking for drug runners and illegal cargo. Police officers at a checkpoint just outside Matamoros, watched as one vehicle drove past them, the male driver seemingly oblivious to them standing there.

A police car followed the vehicle to a nearby ranch and they had a quick look around the property, noting traces of cannabis in several areas. They returned a week later to what they learnt was the Santa Elena Ranch and arrested the driver, Serafin Hernandez, along with his friend, David Valdez, on suspicion of drug trafficking. But in the interrogation room, the two men were cocky and unconcerned. They told the officers that they were under the protection of a power so strong that they could never keep them detained. It turned out that Hernandez did not fail to see the roadblock, but he believed that Constanzo's protection spell rendered him invisible and, therefore, was thoroughly surprised when the police car was able to follow him back to the ranch.

Their defiance would soon be crushed when one of the ranch workers told police that he had seen drug lords and criminals visiting the property. He also mentioned that he had seen a young American and, on the off chance, the officer pulled out a photo of Mark Kilroy. To their shock, the worker identified him as the young man that he had seen.

With ammunition under their belt, they returned to interrogate Hernandez who, realising he was in deep trouble, did not need much persuasion to talk. Not only did he immediately confess to have taken part in the kidnapping and murder of Mark Kilroy but to the officers' surprise, he told them that the American was not the only one. He explained that there had been many more ritualistic killings that had been carried out by the cult he belonged to. To their horror, he described how they captured and killed their victims under the orders of their 'Godfather' Adolfo Constanzo, a dark witch who used the victims' organs and body parts for his rituals. He told them that the bodies were buried on the ranch and police accompanied him there to pinpoint the location.

Several hours later, they stood speechless in front of twelve male corpses that had been buried in a neat row. Mark Kilroy was among them; his skull had been cracked open and his brain removed. He had also been dismembered, as had most of the other corpses.

The barbaric brutality that had been inflicted on the victims was beyond anything the authorities or medical examiners had ever seen. All the victims had been tortured and sodomised before being shot or hacked to death with a machete. Each victim had organs or other body parts missing, with some corpses having been skinned or boiled, possibly alive. Hernandez protested to officials that, while he and others took part in capturing the victims, Constanzo alone had tortured, raped, killed and mutilated them.

As the autopsies were taking place and the victims' families were notified, a team of forensic experts went through every inch of the Santa Elena Ranch with a fine-tooth comb. In a shed, which they soon realised was Constanzo's temple, they discovered a large iron cauldron filled with blood, voodoo ingredients, poisonous insects, animal organs and, to their dismay, Kilroy's brain. Near the cauldron were other satanic witchcraft tools, statues and grisly ornaments such as a necklace made from human vertebrae.

A massive manhunt began to track down the killer witch and his entourage. Time was of the essence; if they did not track him down fast, he had the financial means to flee the country for good. The following weeks were spent searching and following up leads and reports of sightings across the US and South America, all of which produced no results.

By the time officers discovered three additional bodies in an orchard near the ranch, Constanzo was deep in hiding. But he had not left the country. Shortly after Kilroy's murder, having realised that the American's disappearance was not going to fade from the news, he knew he had no choice but to go into hiding. He fled to Mexico City, where he was living between houses and apartments that belonged to his followers. With him were his lovers, Quintana and Orea, a hitman he borrowed from one of his clients nicknamed 'El Duby', and a more recent addition to his harem, Sara Aldrete.

Aldrete was an extremely intelligent Mexican woman with strong academic achievements. At nineteen years of age, she moved back to her family home after a failed marriage and began dating a drug lord. It was through him that she bumped into Constanzo, with whom there was an immediate mutual attraction. A few days later, her boyfriend received an anonymous 'phone call advising him that Aldrete had been cheating on him and, furious, he broke off the relationship. Aldrete fell into Constanzo's arms and they had a torrid sexual affair for a short while, until he tired of her and she realised that he was more attracted to men. By that point, she was already fascinated with his witchcraft and hungrily swallowed every piece of information he taught her about the dark arts. She soon became one of his senior disciples who played an active leadership role within the cult, often coming up with inventive ways to torture their victims, which earned her the title 'La Madrina', meaning the Godmother.

When Constanzo had been forced to go into hiding, Aldrete followed. She had now been in the cult for a few years and her dedication was stronger than ever.

As they prepared to flee Mexico, Constanzo saw a news report on television showing footage of his precious voodoo temple engulfed in flames. On the morning of 22 April 1989, angry locals had set fire to his macabre murder shed that was located on the ranch and the report went on to show police officers supervising a Christian exorcism over the charred remnants. Constanzo was furious. He stormed around the small apartment where they were hiding and smashed every item he could get his hands on, cussing and swearing at his fearful entourage.

Stuck inside the small apartment with an increasingly aggressive sorcerer, Aldrete realised that her life could be in grave danger. She scribbled a note and threw it out of the apartment window.

Please call the judicial police and tell them that in this building are those that they are seeking. Tell them that a woman is being held hostage. I beg for this, because what I want most is to talk.

Her note was of no use as the person who picked it up laughed it off as a prank. But Constanzo's 'protection' would fail him again and, incredibly, it would be yet another coincidence that would lead officers to his lair.

On 6 May 1989, police arrived in the neighbourhood where they were hiding and began to knock on every door, questioning the habitants. In their apartment, Constanzo stood behind a curtain, clutching his machinegun tightly as he watched the officers draw closer to the entrance of their building. Beads of nervous sweat trickled through his thick, black hair and down his neck as his heart pounded faster with their every step.

After a few more minutes, he could take it no longer. He cracked the curtain open, aimed, and began to fire rounds at the law enforcement agents across the street. Within five minutes, over 150 police officers were on the scene, returning fire at the unknown shooter. The residential street became a war zone for nearly forty-five minutes as both sides refused to back down.

If only Constanzo had known that the officers were questioning residents in the area regarding a missing child, he would have most likely made a successful escape from Mexico. But it was too late to back out. Trapped, he knew there were only two options left: surrender, or die. He turned to El Duby, handed him his gun and ordered him to shoot him dead. The hitman hesitated at first; but, when Constanzo flew into a rage, he raised the gun and fired at the witch, just as he pulled his lover Quintana towards him in a tight embrace. The shot rang out across the neighbourhood.

The crossfire suddenly subsided and an eerie silence replaced it. Outside, only one police officer had been injured. Inside, Constanzo and Quintana lay dead, killed by the same bullet. El Duby, Aldrete and Orea were arrested and taken into custody. The nightmare had finally come to an end.

While El Duby confessed immediately, Aldrete attempted to portray herself as a victim who was being held against her will by the cult. But, unwittingly, she gave away details of the crimes when she was in the process of defending herself. The authorities would not be fooled; they soon confirmed that the young woman was, in fact, one of Constanzo's closest assistants who had been actively involved in the murders and other criminal activity that the cult was involved in.

Justice was handed out swiftly. By 1990, the majority of the cult members who had been arrested were sentenced to various prison terms. El Duby received thirty-five years, as did two other cult members who had participated in the ritualistic killings. Constanzo's lover, Orea, died of AIDS before he could receive his sentence and several other cult members were incarcerated for drug trafficking, possession of illegal firearms and obstruction of justice. However, the heaviest sentences were reserved for those who played the most active part in the sadistic murders. Aldrete, despite her pleas of innocence, received sixty-two years imprisonment and two of her colleagues received sixty-seven years. To this day, US authorities are still keeping an eye on the situation as, in the unlikely event that any of the cult members are released from prison, they will be extradited to face trial across the border for the brutal murder of Mark Kilroy.

In all, police connected twenty-three murders to the cult but, they are convinced that there were many more victims. In the years that Constanzo was active, over seventy bodies that bore signs of ritualistic killing, were found in the areas around Mexico City and Matamoros. Fourteen were infants and young children. But a lack of evidence made it impossible to officially charge the cult with those murders and they remain unsolved to this day.

Unlike many cult leaders, Constanzo managed to fill multiple roles in a controlled and organised manner. At the height of his criminal career he was a drug lord, crime godfather, satanic witch and cult leader. Looking back at his childhood, it is not difficult to see how he became the perverse man that he was. He had been raised from birth totally immersed in an obscure religion, with hardly any outside influence or education. From a young age, he was told that he was superior to other human beings and possessed mystical powers. He was desensitised to suffering, having been made to watch his mother and his priest kill animals and mutilate their bodies for use in their cauldrons. It is said that, as a child, his mother would reward him for good behaviour by allowing him to slaughter an animal that was destined for one of her upcoming rituals.

He must have believed that he was invincible. Ironically, however, both incidents that led to his demise were pure coincidence and off the back of completely unrelated police activities. His protective spells were clearly ineffective on both occasions.

It is not known whether the Haitian priest he spent time with as a young teenager was a paedophile, though it is not impossible to imagine that he groomed Constanzo, given that they spent the majority of their time together alone. A sexually abusive relationship with his mentor could also explain his aggression towards his male victims and the acts of sodomy and torture that he inflicted on them. Nevertheless, there is no excuse for the horrific pain and suffering he caused his victims before killing them. He was truly a sadist who had absolutely no empathy or emotion towards those he murdered. I do not believe he was insane; to the contrary, he demonstrated high levels of intelligence and the capacity to not only control and manipulate people, but to run a very profitable criminal organisation.

Following his death there were rumours that, before Aldrete, Constanzo had mentored another woman who became the cult's first godmother. It is said that she was never discovered and was, therefore, able to gather a following and continue his work undetected. Whether that is true or not will most likely remain a mystery. I truly believe that evil of such magnitude cannot go unpunished forever and if she does exist, her judgement will come, in this life or the next, just as it did for Constanzo. He believed that he could control fate, but ironically it was a twist of fate that caused his downfall. I am certain that his victims are resting in peace, just as I am certain that he is burning in the fires of hell.

CHAPTER 9

Prophet Of Death:
Jeffrey Lundgren

Jeffrey Lundgren was born on 3 May 1950 in Missouri and was raised in a family that were zealous followers of the RLDS Church (Reorganised Church of Jesus Christ of Latter Day Saints), which emerged from the Mormon Church. His father had a well-paid job in construction, while his mother was a house-proud, stay-at-home mother, who dedicated her time and energy into raising her children and embellishing their image in the community. This seemingly perfect family unit was just a front. Lundgren later revealed that, throughout his early childhood, he was terribly abused by his violent father as his mother watched on, never making a move to defend him.

In his adolescent years, he became a loner, spending most of his time isolated from his peers and lost in his own thoughts. One neighbour claimed to have seen him nail a small rabbit to a piece of wood and beat it to death when he was a young teenager. Such a heartless act of animal cruelty is often found in the childhood of murderers and serial killers. He grew close to his father as a teenager when he showed an interest in hunting, which was his father's preferred hobby. They often went on hunting trips together and his father passed on his expert shooting techniques, which resulted in Lundgren becoming an excellent hunter himself.

Following high school, he enrolled at Central Missouri State University and, during his time there, he frequented a RLDS youth house where he met Alice Keeler. She, too, had suffered abuse from her father throughout her childhood and, before long, their friendship turned into a love affair, which resulted in them both dropping out of college when Keeler became pregnant in 1969. They married in 1970 and Lundgren enlisted in the US Navy shortly after.

In December 1970, their first son was born and, by 1974, his wife was expecting another boy. Lundgren requested an early release from his four-year term as an electronics technician with the US Navy, claiming that his wife could not cope with his absence any longer. He eventually received an honorable discharge, allowing him to return home just after the birth of his second child.

He moved his family to San Diego but they struggled to make ends meet, forcing them to return to Missouri where his wife gave birth to their third child, a daughter, in 1979. Both Lundgren and his wife remained active members of the RLDS Church, but their financial situation was volatile as he could not keep a job for more than a few weeks at a time due to his inability to accept authority. With three young children and financial difficulties, their marriage began to suffer. Lundgren, who had always had problems with infidelity, was growing tired of his wife and allegedly became abusive towards both her and their children at this point. It is claimed he pushed her down the stairs, causing her to have to undergo emergency surgery for a ruptured spleen. In a desperate bid to save her marriage, she became pregnant almost immediately after the birth of her daughter and their fourth child, another son, was born in 1980.

The following year, things seemed to take a positive turn when Lundgren was offered the post of Lay Minister at his local church. It was during this time that he became interested in creating his own following. He studied the scriptures word for word, searching for patterns and verses to back up the bizarre doctrines he was creating.

He initially had just a handful of followers; some were friends from university, while others were RLDS members who had also grown disillusioned with the church. They gave him money and attended his Bible classes, but soon that was not enough for Lundgren. His greedy nature prompted him to move to Kirtland, Ohio and, once there, he and his wife visited the revered Kirtland Temple, which was managed by the RLDS. Shortly after they arrived, they were offered the position of temple guides in exchange for free room and board behind the temple and a very small weekly wage.

Lundgren relished his role as a guide as it enabled him to share his interpretation of the scriptures with the visitors that passed through. But the reality of their financial situation was impossible to ignore. Such a small wage was not enough to live on and, before long, Lundgren was dipping into the temple's donations and profits, stealing an estimated $25,000 during the time he was working there.

As he had done in Missouri, Lundgren began preaching from his home. He attracted a small circle of devoted followers who were enthralled with his knowledge of the Bible and the Book of Mormon. He impressed them with his ability to quote large sections of both books entirely from memory and they revered him as a prophet. They were drawn in by his false claim that he had created chiastic interpretation. This was a doctrine founded on the principle that all things created by God had two sides—the left, and the right, which was the mirror of the left just as the left side of the Kirtland Temple was a mirror of the right. He claimed that this applied to Bible scriptures as well, explaining to his followers that, for a sentence in the scriptures to be confirmed as the truth, the sentences above and below it had to 'mirror' it and be consistent with its meaning. This allowed him great flexibility in his interpretation of the Bible and the doctrines he created as a result grew further and further from the standard teachings of Christianity.

In 1987, Lundgren was fired from his role as temple guide due to suspicions of theft and they evicted him from his church-owned housing. He and his family rented a farmhouse in the area and some of his most devoted followers moved in with them. His male disciples worked in various jobs and handed over their paychecks to Lundgren, while the women helped with household chores and took care of the children. Those who moved into the house were Kevin Currie, Danny Kraft, Sharon Bluntschly, Richard Brand, Greg Winship and Debbie Olivarez. Three other families were also a part of his flock and, although they were just as devout as his live-in members, they chose to retain their own residences. Those were Dennis and Tonya Patrick, Ronald and Susan Luff and Dennis and Cheryl Avery.

Over time, Lundgren's teachings became increasingly depraved. He stepped up his level of control over members and began to make references to perverse sexual acts during his sermons. He utilised mind control over them, forbidding them to speak to one another in private and spying on any conversations he heard, later using the information to 'prove' that he could read their minds. One of his followers, Kevin Currie, soon had enough and abandoned the cult.

Shortly after Currie's departure, perhaps in a bid to renew his flock's dedication, Lundgren revealed two dates for the second coming of Christ, which he claimed to have received in a vision. He told his followers that Christ would slay all human beings, apart from the chosen righteous who would be safe in the Kirtland Temple. Once the two dates had passed and nothing had happened, Lundgren knew that he had to quickly come up with a new plan. He told his followers that, in another vision, he had received an instruction from God that they were to take control of the Kirtland Temple on 3 May, which was his birthday. He did not specify a year but, together, they went on to formulate a plan which involved executing RLDS Church officials and residents in the surrounding area, including anyone who got in their way on the chosen day. This killing spree would be called the 'cleansing' and, according to Lundgren, would be the event that would trigger the apocalypse. They began to put their plan into action. They purchased weapons and underwent combat training, lead by Lundgren's eldest son Damon, who was just seventeen. They watched violent movies to pick up tips, studied military tactics and analysed maps of the area.

Around this time, Currie returned to the fold after begging Lundgren to take him back. Perhaps their radical new plan was the bait he needed to be pulled back into the cult. In 1988, the RLDS Church officially excommunicated Lundgren, which only gave him a deeper hatred for their denomination, adding fuel to an already explosive situation.

Meanwhile, Dennis and Cheryl Avery, along with their three daughters, moved from Missouri, where they had initially joined Lundgren's cult, to Kirtland. Unbeknownst to the Averys, the Lundgren family strongly disliked them. They openly criticised Dennis for not controlling his children sufficiently and for allowing his wife to make decisions in the household. They also chastised them regularly for any sins that they felt they had committed and intentionally failed to invite them to many of their meetings. Jeffrey Lundgren admitted to his wife that the only reason he allowed the Averys into his group was for financial gain. The Averys had sold their property in Missouri for $19,000 and rented accommodation in Kirtland. Sure enough, after putting pressure on the couple, they gave in and handed $10,000 over to Lundgren, who assured them that, in return, he would look after them.

Around this time, Shar Lea Olsen, a friend of cult members Brand and Winship, joined the cult and moved into the communal home. In early 1989, Currie yet again became disillusioned with Lundgren's fanatical doctrines and he left the cult. But this time, he did not bid them farewell and walk out the front door; he fled in secret, covering his tracks out of fear for his life. And he was right to do so. After all, he knew everything about their explosive plan to hijack the Kirtland Temple and, if the cult tracked him down, he feared that they would be prepared to go to any lengths to silence him. In a panic, he called the FBI and told them what was taking place at the farmhouse. They did not believe him but, as a precaution, they passed the information on to the Kirtland authorities who began an investigation. Lundgren was fuming when he realised that Currie had betrayed him yet again and his anger reached boiling point when Olsen left the community as well. When she returned to her family, she told them that she feared for her life, and that she was certain that she would end up dead or imprisoned if she did not leave the cult.

Panicked that he was losing control, Lundgren cranked up the intensity of the sessions he held with his followers. He wore army fatigues daily and carried a loaded gun with him at all times, which he kept visible at his side when he was preaching. He also turned almost any action into a serious sin; even adding too much seasoning to food was considered a transgression. But, above all, keeping your own money for yourself became utterly unacceptable. In a bid to solidify the unity of his troupes, Lundgren instructed the union of four of his disciples. He performed the wedding ceremonies himself, pairing Bluntschly with Brand and Winship with Olivarez. He also celebrated the arrival of long-term friends Larry and Kathy Johnson and their four children, who moved into the communal home with them.

Just after their arrival, Lundgren revealed a new plan to his flock. The Kirtland Temple attack was cancelled as God had told him that they had another target, the increasingly doubtful Avery family, whom he resented for not having turned over the remaining profit from the sale of their house. He told his followers that by 'purging the troops' and offering the Averys as sacrifices, they would all be cleansed and would be allowed to enter God's presence. But he warned them that they had to be prepared to flee into the wilderness following the cleansing. Those with jobs resigned, credit cards were maxed-out purchasing supplies, and families began packing their belongings in preparation for their departure.

Amidst the hubbub of activity surrounding the move, Lundgren instructed a few of his men to begin digging a pit into the floor of the old red barn located on their property. They were given instructions to never be seen near the barn when Dennis Avery was visiting. It took them four days to dig the pit, which measured six-by-seven-foot and was four feet deep.

Lundgren told the Avery family that the whole group would be going on a wilderness retreat and that they should make preparations to leave with them. He told Cheryl Avery to write letters to their relatives, letting them know that they were moving to Wyoming so that they would not worry. The Averys followed Lundgren's instructions and, on 17 April 1989, they moved their belongings to the farmhouse and checked into a nearby motel that Lundgren had booked for them; they believed that they would be travelling with the others to the retreat the following day. That night, they all had dinner together at the farmhouse. Apart from the innocent family of five, everyone in the house knew that the Avery's would not survive the night. The plan was in motion and Lundgren's followers had all sworn to follow through with it. As soon as dinner was over, Lundgren's male disciples followed him to the barn, where he explained that they were to lure each member of the Avery family there one by one, where they would then be bound, gagged and thrown in to the pit before their execution. Ronald Luff exited the barn and moved towards the house as the others hid in their positions, ready to strike. He told Dennis Avery that he needed help to prepare some equipment for their journey into the wilderness the following day. The middle-aged father agreed and followed him out into the foggy night.

When they entered the barn, Luff tried to immobilise him using a stun gun, but it only produced a low voltage electrical shock that weakened Dennis though he was still fully conscious. He was acutely aware of the danger that he was in and he cried out, begging for his life, but it was to no avail. Brand and Kraft moved out of the shadows to play their part; one held him down, while the other bound and gagged him with duct tape. They threw him into the pit where he thrashed about, trying to free himself and continuing to plead with his captors through muffled cries. Lundgren sat on a pile of dirt near the pit, gun in hand, watching his victim struggle for his life.

Standing outside the barn, Winship revved up the chainsaw in order to mask the sound of the gunfire, while Lundgren raised his gun and shot Dennis twice in the back. His victim slumped into the dirt of the pit, where he took his last breaths. 'You had better see what this looks like!' Lundgren called out to his men. They filed past, each glancing in the pit as ordered.

Luff went into the house again, this time for Cheryl Avery. He told her that her husband was looking for her and she followed him to the barn, leaving her three daughters happily playing games in the living room and chatting excitedly with the other children about the planned adventure that they were embarking on the next day. The other women in the house kept an eye on the children, all the while knowing exactly what was taking place outside.

As Cheryl entered the barn, Luff used the stun gun, which yet again failed to render their victim unconscious. As Cheryl began to panic, Lundgren placed a hand on her shoulder and told her to stop struggling and relax as it would be easier that way. Knowing that she had no chance of escape and seeing what they had done to her husband, she resigned herself to her fate. She stopped struggling and let her body fall limply to the ground as the men bound her. They coaxed her into the dirt pit and the signal was given to start the chainsaw again. Lundgren shot her three times, twice in the breast area and once in the stomach. She died next to her beloved husband's body, unaware that her killers would not even have the mercy to spare her children.

Luff returned to the house and lured fifteen-year-old Trina Avery out under the pretense that they were going to play hide and seek. When they reached the barn, she stood frozen in shock as they bound her and lay her down in the pit. Lundgren aimed at her head and fired, but he missed and the bullet skimmed past her head. Her survival instincts kicked in and she began to scream out in fear before the second bullet hit her in the head and she died instantly. Not one man expressed shock or sorrow as they witnessed the young girl die. They had a job to finish and they carried on with the killings as if it were a mundane chore.

Luff went back to the house a third time, this time for thirteen-year-old Becky Avery. To lure her out, he told her that he would take her to see some horses. Once in the barn, they followed the same process, binding and gagging the child before laying her on top of her mother's body in the pit. Two shots were fired; one of which hit her in the chest. An eerie silence filled the barn, broken only by the gurgling sounds emerging from the pit as Becky, still alive, struggled to breathe. Lundgren did not even have the mercy to shoot her again and put her out of her misery. Instead, he left her there to die alone in the blood-soaked pit, as they prepared for the final killing.

Six-year-old Karen Avery did not stand a chance. She, too, was lured out with the promise that she would see horses, and Luff playfully carried her to the scene of her death. She was bound and lowered into the pit next the bodies of her family. As the chainsaw roared outside, two shots were fired. The second one hit her in the head, killing her instantly.

Two hours later, the floor of the barn was level again; Lundgren's men had poured a limestone mixture over the bodies before burying them to cover up the smell of decomposition. The Averys' belongings had been retrieved from the motel, erasing all trace that they were ever there.

The following day, as cult members were frantically packing and preparing to leave, police officers arrived at the farmhouse to question Lundgren following the information that the FBI had received from Currie. They had set up occasional surveillance on the farmhouse, which unfortunately was not in place the night before, and they had seen nothing suspicious. The group denied all knowledge of a plan to attack the Kirtland Temple and refuted all of Currie's allegations. Without evidence, the authorities had no choice but to leave.

As soon as they had gone, Lundgren and his followers fled the farmhouse and began their journey to the wilderness. They settled in a campsite near Davis, West Virginia, and there they kept a low profile, living in tents until October. Some took on jobs and others continued their internal military training as they waited for Lundgren to announce their next move. During their stay in West Virginia, dissention began to fester in the group. Lundgren had infuriated several of his men when he decided to help himself to their wives. First he chose Tonya Patrick, but the arrangement did not work out and he returned her to her husband, pregnant with his child. He then chose Kathryn Johnson, who became his second wife, much to the dismay of her husband, Larry Johnson. She, too, was soon pregnant with the cult leader's child.

When Lundgren decided to move back to Missouri in October, more disagreements occurred and, by December, Larry Johnson had seen and heard enough. He contacted federal law enforcement authorities and told them about the murders and where they could find the bodies. Over the following weeks, five other cult members also left Lundgren.

On the frozen winter morning of 3 January 1990, Kirtland police arrived at the location that Johnson had given them and they began the gruesome task of digging up the floor of the barn. As they dug, the stench that filled the air was one that they immediately recognised as human decomposition. They found Dennis Avery's body first and, not long after, that of his wife. To their dismay, they confirmed the truth of Johnson's tip-off when they found the bodies of the couple's three young daughters. Many police officers on the scene could not handle the discovery and were physically sick, or broke down into floods of tears.

As they tried to piece together the events that had led to the five murders, arrest warrants were issued and, one by one, over the next few weeks, members of Lundgren's cult were arrested and taken in for questioning. The cult leader and his family went on the run, but authorities were fast on his tail in a nationwide manhunt. They found him close to the Mexican border and arrested him, his first wife, Alice, and his nineteen-year-old son Damon, who had played a key part in the killings. Lundgren was charged with five counts of murder and five counts of kidnapping.

Following a series of interviews, the truth of what had occurred that fateful night in April came to light. Lundgren was unapologetic and continued to claim that he had no choice but to kill the Avery family, as God had told him to do so. His wife, Alice, seemed emotionally detached to the whole situation and she dismissed police when questioned, telling them that they should ask her husband about that night. During an interrogation, a cult member revealed that, as the killings were taking place, Lundgren had acted as though they were a biology experiment, shooting the victims in different parts of their bodies to see which died quickest. It became clear that there was no limit to Lundgren's depraved mind. Had he not been caught when he had, there was no telling how many more people he would have killed.

The trial began on 23 August 1990 and, six days later, after just two hours of deliberation, the jury returned a guilty verdict on all counts. In September, he was given the maximum sentence. The justice department showed him no mercy and he was sentenced to death by lethal injection. Alice Lundgren received five life sentences and their son, Damon, received four. Both will never see the outside of a prison again. Ten other cult members were also tried and sentenced according to their level of involvement in the murders. The cold demeanour of Ronald Luff earned him the heaviest punishment of them all, with a sentence of 170 years to life. The following year, Alice filed for divorce but Kathryn Johnson remained loyal to Lundgren.

Despite numerous appeals, the state of Ohio carried out Jeffrey Lundgren's execution on 24 October 2006. His final meal was turkey, potatoes, gravy and salad, with a pumpkin pie and whipped cream for dessert. A couple of hours prior to his execution, he spoke to his ex-wife, Alice, on the 'phone and broke down in tears, but I very much doubt that they were tears of regret as, in his final statement, he professed his love for his second wife, Kathryn, and made absolutely no mention of his victims. He did not show any signs of remorse; to the end, he was cold as steel, unapologetic and steadfast in his insane belief that he was carrying out God's work.

At 10:26 am he was pronounced dead by lethal injection. The old red barn was demolished the following year, erasing all trace of the tragedy that had occurred there.

CHAPTER 10

The Branch Davidians: David Koresh

It was an event that dominated the media across the United States for fifty-one days. Nearly two months of siege crawled by in slow motion as the FBI surrounded the Branch Davidian ranch just outside of Waco, Texas, with neither side prepared to give in. Behind closed doors, it was a battle of minds; David Koresh versus the FBI negotiation team.

It was a dangerous game, one that could cost the lives of nearly eighty souls trapped in the ranch, and it was a standoff that would have a devastating end.

David Koresh was born Vernon Wayne Howell on 17 August 1959 in Houston, Texas. His mother was fifteen-year-old Bonnie Sue Clark who had fallen pregnant by her boyfriend, Bobby Howell. Before Clark gave birth, Howell met and fell in love with another teenage girl and promptly abandoned the young, expectant mother and their unborn child.

Koresh never met his father, but his mother soon became involved with another man and moved in with him. He was a violent alcoholic who was often abusive to both mother and child. Koresh was just four years of age when his mother's tumultuous relationship ended and she left him in the care of her mother, Earline, who lived in the Dallas suburb of Garland. Koresh's grandmother immediately introduced him to her beloved Church of the Seventh Day Adventists and they attended every fellowship meeting without fail. His mother eventually returned three years later with a new husband, carpenter Roy Halderman. Another child was on the way and his half-brother, Roger, was born shortly after.

Due to his dyslexia and slow capacity to learn, Koresh was often a reject at school and a very lonesome child. He was eventually placed in special education classes, which only deteriorated his social position among his peers. He was targeted by bullies who nicknamed him 'Mister Retardo' and it was later alleged that he was gang-raped by older boys when he was just eight years old. By the time he reached High School he had lost all hope of becoming an achiever in life and he dropped out of junior year, taking up a job in carpentry.

In his early twenties, it is rumoured he impregnated a fifteen-year-old girl and then abandoned her to move to Los Angeles, in an attempt to launch a career as a rock star. He failed, and when he returned to Houston he joined his mother's Seventh Day Adventist Church. Not long after, he fell in love with the pastor's daughter and, despite warnings to keep away, continued to harass her, which resulted in his excommunication from the church. Koresh then moved on to join the Branch Davidians in 1981, regularly participating in services at their headquarters, the Mount Carmel Center in Waco, Texas.

The Branch Davidians are a religious group that was founded by former members of the Seventh Day Adventist Church after their membership was cancelled due to their messianic and more fanatical religious views. Their leader at this time was Lois Roden, whose husband Ben Roden, had led the group for over twenty years. When he died in 1978, his son George tried to take over leadership; however, he was soon pushed out of the running by his mother, who had spent the years prior to her husband's death carefully manoeuvring her way into a position that would allow her to take control. She had begun by revealing that she was a prophetess and, soon after, announced that the Holy Spirit was female in gender, thus ensuring that, when the time came, it would be perfectly acceptable for a woman to take over the leadership of the group. It worked and she was elected as President of the Church.

When Koresh first arrived he attempted to share his own revelations, but he was ignored. He persisted over the following two years, returning again and again until he realised that his only chance of success would lie in forming a closer relationship with the leader of the church. It was alleged that he began a sexual affair with seventy-seven-year-old Lois Roden, whom he seduced by persuading her that God had chosen him to impregnate her with the Chosen One. With her judgement swayed, Roden allowed Koresh to preach his own message, even promoting his spiritual gifts to her followers, which sparked discontent amongst certain members of the church.

Needless to say, George Roden was seething. After being upstaged by his mother, he was now yet again, waiting in line to become the leader of the group. But he felt increasingly threatened by Koresh's presence and furious that he had managed to worm his way into his mother's good favours. With tensions rising, Koresh made a move to calm the situation when he announced that God had instructed him to marry fourteen-year-old teenager, Rachel Jones. They were wed shortly after in 1984 and she went on to bear him a son and two daughters.

But it was not enough to soothe the rising tension and, shortly after, George Roden and a group of his supporters drove Koresh off the ranch at gunpoint.

He and twenty-four of his disciples were exiled and they travelled 90 miles to Palestine, Texas, where they lived in rough conditions for the following two years, finding refuge in tents and vehicles.

At some point during this period, Koresh visited Israel, where he claimed to have had a vision that he was the new Cyrus, a Persian king who had allowed the Jews to return to their homeland. He also claimed that he had unlocked the Seven Seals within the Book of Revelation which are, according to the Bible, the mysterious events that will lead to the apocalypse. They are mysterious because the passages contain symbols that, as with so many passages in the Bible, appear to be coded or to hold a meaning that is left open to interpretation. Bible scholars have studied these passages for centuries to no avail and yet Koresh convinced his followers that he had unlocked its secrets.

He told them that God had commissioned him to establish the Davidic Kingdom in Jerusalem and prophesied that he would be the one to trigger the events that would bring about the end of the world. He added that it was his destiny to die as a martyr in Jerusalem. The apocalypse as he described it would include great destruction and fire that would cause many deaths. It is a description that is eerily similar to the blaze that would consume many of his followers years later.

When he returned to Texas, he set about recruiting as many disciples as he could. Simultaneously, and despite his physical distance from Davidian headquarters, he managed to increase the number of followers that he had in Waco to such an extent that, by the time Lois Roden died in 1986, he had won over the majority of the church. As expected, George Roden was furious. In a desperate attempt to keep his position, he challenged Koresh to a spiritual duel. He exhumed a corpse and hid it, and then claimed that he had resurrected the occupant of the empty grave and challenged Koresh to do likewise. Koresh discovered what he had done and seized the opportunity to get rid of Roden by informing the police, but they told him he had to have evidence if was going to make such a claim.

He did not hesitate. Armed and accompanied by seven of his men, he stormed through the Mount Carmel Center grounds in a bid to take photographs of the crime. Roden's men intercepted them and a gunfight ensued, which resulted in Roden suffering a minor gunshot wound to one of his fingers. Because of this, Koresh and his men were tried for attempted murder. But when they explained they were on a mission to find evidence of a crime, they avoided conviction.

By 1989, Roden had but a handful of followers left and he was in a fragile mental state. When he slaughtered a man with an axe for claiming to be the messiah, he was convicted of murder and sent to a mental institution. Koresh was finally free to proclaim himself the leader of the Branch Davidians.

In 1990, he legally changed his name to David Koresh—David to symbolise his belief that he was a direct descendant of the biblical King David, and Koresh as the translation for Cyrus, the Persian king who, he believed, he was the reincarnation of. Children who were raised in the cult later said that Koresh had also claimed that his last name represented the final breath of a human being before they die. His transformation was complete and he had now taken on a new persona. He was no longer a mere mortal but a powerful prophet, on a divine mission from God.

He began to build on his initial prophecies, taking them further into obscurity over time as so often occurs when a cult leader obtains full power over his flock. His vision of the Davidic Kingdom was slightly altered when he revealed to his followers that he would no longer be martyred in Jerusalem but in the US, and that the Davidic Kingdom would be set up at their own headquarters, at the Mount Carmel Center in Waco, Texas.

He then introduced a doctrine called the 'House of David', which involved him setting up spiritual marriages between himself and some of the married and single women in the church. According to his revelation, God had instructed him to select 'chosen' women in the community with whom he would produce twenty-four children. These youngsters would grow up to become the ruling elders during the Millennium, following the return of Christ. The women selected, if married, would have their marriages spiritually annulled by Koresh so that he could informally wed them and add them to his growing harem. However, he ordered his male followers to take vows of celibacy and, needless to say, for some of his disciples this was a bridge too far. Several husbands refused to participate or to give up their wives and they left the compound with their families, unaware of just how close they had been to a horrific death. But most remained mesmerised by their charismatic leader and willing to follow him down any path he chose to take them.

Following this revelation, Koresh produced at least twelve offspring out of wedlock. There were also allegations that this sexual policy included under-aged girls. The only instance that could be verified was his spiritual marriage to his wife Rachel's younger sister, Michelle, who was thirteen years of age when the mock wedding ceremony was performed. Another girl came forward years later, alleging that the perverse leader had forced her to perform sex acts on him from the age of ten.

Shortly after, Koresh announced another one of his revelations that would play a key part in the events that would later unfold. He told his followers that God had instructed him to build an army as the apocalypse was imminent. He prophesied that the US army would launch an attack on Mount Carmel and that they, as the chosen ones, were ordained by God to fight them in what would be the final days before the end of world. If they did so, they would be guaranteed direct access to heaven. As part of their plan, they had to be prepared to defend themselves and, in order to do so, they began stockpiling ammunition for self-defence and also stored up large quantities of food. To raise extra cash, Koresh began buying and selling guns at local gun fairs in the area. He also instructed the construction of a 'bunker', which was a school bus that was buried in the earth on their property.

As the preparations continued, one disgruntled ex-member, Marc Breault, went to the authorities alleging that, behind the closed doors of Mount Carmel, children were being beaten and sexual abuse was taking place with minors. He also told authorities that Koresh and his men were stockpiling ammunition and were in possession of illegal weapons. The ATF (US Bureau of Alcohol, Tobacco and Firearms) was called into the investigation and their agents were immediately concerned that something sinister was taking place in the compound.

The ATF sent undercover agents to the Mount Carmel Center to act as young students who were interested in Koresh's teachings and they set up round-the-clock surveillance of the property. A few months later, they felt that they had enough evidence to request a warrant to search the property for illegal weapons, and to arrest Koresh for questioning. The warrant was granted and they put in place a plan to raid the property by surprise. However, on the morning it was due to take place, one of their moles informed them that Koresh had been made aware of the impending raid. Having lost the element of surprise, they moved quickly.

Just before 10 a.m. on the morning of 28 February 1993, over seventy ATF agents surrounded Mount Carmel as three of their helicopters circled the sky above the ranch. As they closed in, gunfire was exchanged. The Davidians and conspiracy theorists vehemently claim to this day that the ATF began shooting first and that the cult only shot back in self-defence. The ATF maintains that the Davidians started the exchange, but what we do know as a fact, regardless of who shot first, is that this was the start of an ordeal that no one could have imagined would have lasted the fifty-one long days that it did.

The gunfire was relentless, with both sides shooting to kill as dozens of women and children cowered fearfully in the back rooms of the buildings. By noon, the longest gunfight in American law enforcement history came to an end. The ATF called a truce. They were beaten and they withdrew with sixteen wounded and the bodies of four agents who were killed in the shoot-out. Within the walls of the compound, six were dead and many were injured. Koresh had been shot in the abdomen and wrist when, according to Davidian survivors, he opened the front door in an attempt to reason with the ATF swat team. The ATF claims that the door was never opened and, therefore, Koresh must have obtained his injuries by being hit by a stray bullet that went through the door. Among the community trapped in the property, there were several trained nurses who were able to treat wounded cult members and Koresh recovered from his injuries in the weeks that followed.

As over a hundred Davidians barricaded themselves in Mount Carmel, the FBI Hostage Rescue team arrived on the scene and set up a command post. Lead negotiator, Byron Sage, was one of the first on site and, despite his many years of experience, he knew instantly that this stand-off would not be easily solved. Tension was high on both sides and he got to work immediately. His first goal was to establish a relationship with the man that he knew was solely in control of the commune and the only one who had the power to decide how this conflict would end, namely David Koresh.

The negotiation team's primary concern lay with the children who were stuck in the middle of this dangerous situation. After over an hour of conversation with the negotiators, Koresh offered them a deal. If they would broadcast over local radio, a selection of biblical verses that he had chosen, then he would release the children. It seemed too good to be true; such a small request in exchange for all the children was a bargain for the FBI and they agreed. As the scriptures were read out over the air, the story of the Waco siege was breaking news worldwide. The pressure was on for the negotiators to deliver positive news to the press and the families of those involved.

With the broadcast over, Koresh began to carry out his side of the bargain. Sent out in pairs, the release spilled into the following day with a total of fourteen children exiting the building. But then, Koresh made another demand. He told negotiators he wanted to record a message that would be broadcasted to the entire nation. Negotiators were hesitant but with so many children still inside, they made a deal with him. If they played his message nationwide, he and all of his followers had to surrender peacefully as soon the broadcast was over. On the third day, as Davidians packed and prepared to come out, Koresh's voice echoed across the country on morning radio shows. However, as the recording came to a close, there was no sign of anyone leaving the property. They waited all afternoon with only one message from the compound when Koresh assured them that the plan was proceeding but that he wanted to lead his people in prayer first.

They continued to wait but, by 6 p.m., they knew something was not right. They called Steve Schneider, Koresh's right-hand man, and asked him what the situation was.

> Steve: 'Er, I just talked to him and he's been going through a lot of anguish and what the guy just went through, I've never seen anything like it before. But he wanted me to remind you to read Psalms chapter 2.'

Negotiator: 'Steve, but what is this...?' (Steve cuts him off)

Steve: 'Everything is ready to go right now but all of a sudden he started praying.'

It was the worst news that the negotiators could receive. Koresh had changed his mind and it seemed that he was not prepared to release any more of his people.

Negotiator: 'He gave us his word.'

Steve: 'I know that, I'm aware of that. But what if there is a higher power than you or I that speaks to an individual? Be aware of who you're dealing with.'

Negotiator: 'Just remember that David told the world that he was coming out.'

Steve: 'I understand that. Can I read Revelation 18 to you now?'

Negotiator: 'Steve, I want him to come out.'

Steve: 'He says his God says that he is to wait.'

The assault team was furious. Team Operator Jim McGee and his men were baffled as to why they were not being given the green light for one of their snipers to take down Koresh, in light of the failed negotiation. They were sure that Koresh would not give in and that a full-on assault was the solution; they were confident that their unit could provide just that. But senior FBI agents had decided to trust the negotiation team and, rather than order an assault, they instructed the assault team to station their tanks around the property in the hope that the Branch Davidians would be intimidated.

Under increasing pressure to produce results, the negotiators upped their efforts to save as many of the children as they could, successfully negotiating the release of seven more over the next few days. But, by the second week, there were still around twenty children in the compound. The negotiators sent a box of milk into the compound with a listening device hidden inside. What they heard was deeply concerning, but it gave them a glimpse into the mental state of the cult leader.

Koresh: 'Rachel! Keep those children under control. They won't be singing that today. We need to send some guys up there and blow their heads off.'

In an attempt to reignite a relationship with Koresh, the negotiators sent him a video recorder and, a few hours later, a tape was sent back. In the video clip, Koresh introduced several of his children and he smiles as he converses with them, portraying the image of a loving and tender parent with his offspring.

Negotiators felt that this exchange was a step forward and that perhaps there was still a chance to achieve a positive outcome, but the assault team had other ideas. Frustrated with the time it was taking to bring the siege to a close, they decided to take action. They cut off the property's electricity supply and the commune was instantly deprived of heat and running water in the freezing temperatures of early spring.

The negotiators were enraged. The assault team had severely damaged, if not destroyed, the line of communication with Koresh that they had worked so hard to build. Had the situation not been so serious it would have been almost laughable—the alpha males of the FBI versus a self-appointed messiah, with the negotiators caught in the middle, playing the role of referee. Gone was reason; it was now a battle of egos.

The negotiation team knew that the stand-off had turned into precisely the situation that they were trying to avoid. They knew there was now almost no chance that the Davidians would exit the compound by their own volition. In a desperate bid to maintain a connection, they sent Koresh a videotape of themselves, introducing their wives and children by means of photographs. By showing that they, too, were family men they were attempting to appeal to the parental nature of the Davidians, in the hope that their love for their offspring would prompt them to release the remaining children. But their efforts were in vain. Koresh appeared to have no desire to communicate further and he withdrew into his increasingly troubled thoughts. Local Sheriff Harwell, who had met Koresh on several occasions, was called in to try and reopen communication with the Davidians.

To their surprise, Koresh agreed to meet with the sheriff to talk about a resolution. Under the cover of snipers, negotiator Byron Sage and the sheriff met Steve Schneider and Koresh's second right-hand man, Wayne Martin, just outside the compound. The air was so tense it was tangible, but the conversation appeared to be a success and they parted with Steve's promise that they would relay everything that had been said to Koresh. This was confirmed in a recording that their bug picked up later that evening.

> Steve: 'Byron, I liked. Man, what a person. I liked his personality. I believe he was one hundred per cent sincere. I believe what he is trying to do.'

But Koresh was not prepared to give in just yet. A handful of his followers had left the compound in the last week and, worried that his men may turn against him, he put a stop to any further meetings. Communications ground to a halt once more. But then, on a frosty morning, without warning, seven Davidians were seen exiting the compound. Some were mothers, desperate to be reunited with their children, while others were cult members that were exhausted with the situation and no longer prepared to be a part of it. It was a huge accomplishment for the negotiators. However, yet again, the tactical assault team took matters into their own hands. Still unsatisfied with the results that the negotiating team had delivered, they launched an assault on the compound. Their tanks approached the building, crushing vehicles and outdoor sheds in their path. The Davidians were appalled; they had allowed seven people out and, in return, their property was being torn apart.

Through Schneider, the negotiators tried everything they could to keep the communication line open, but the assault team would not let up. In a bid to weaken the cult members' resolve by sleep deprivation, they began pumping mind-numbing music into the compound whilst shining floodlights through the windows. The sound of animal cries, sirens, bagpipes and Tibetan Buddhist chanting rang out day and night. In response, Koresh set up an amplifier and played rock music at maximum volume.

Yet again, the stand-off had turned into a farce but, this time, both sides were reaching the end of their tether. Byron Sage's colleague, negotiator Gary Noesner, who had been on the team since day one, left on day twenty-six, certain that there was now nothing more that could be done to salvage the situation. He was right. Only one Davidian walked out of Mount Carmel between that day and the last.

Things ground to a halt from that point on; it was as if time stood still for the next three weeks. In the frosty fields that surrounded the compound, the FBI watched and waited while the Davidians remained holed up in their sanctuary. On day forty-six, Koresh finally broke his silence, making one last offer to the negotiators. He told Sage that he would come out in two weeks, when he had finished the manuscript that he was writing about the meaning of the seven seals, the apocalyptic seals that are described in the Book of Revelation. Negotiators agreed but, as expected, the assault team was not happy. They believed that this was just another of Koresh's tricks to buy time. Over the next few days, the cult prophet ranted a tirade of scriptures to the negotiation team over the 'phone, wasting precious time that was meant to be spent on completing his manuscript.

The FBI's patience had run out. A plan was put in place that was approved at the highest levels of government and, on day fifty-one, the assault team moved into position. At 6 a.m. on the cold, dark morning of 19 April 1993, negotiator Byron Sage called the number that he had dialled so many times in the last few weeks and Steve Schneider answered the call.

Byron Sage: 'We're in the process of placing tear gas into the building.'

Steve immediately hung up, but the recording device picked up the panic that was rising in the compound.

Unknown male: 'Everybody grab your masks! Everybody grab your masks!'
Unknown female: 'I need a mask! I need a mask!'

Outside, the FBI tanks loaded with CS gas approached the compound. Within minutes, a flurry of gunfire erupted from the windows, crashing through the silence of dawn. Helicopters circled the area as the tanks closed in. Their initial intent had been to release the gas in small doses over two days; however, as the situation had already escalated, they were forced to change tactics and, after approval from their superiors, they prepared to insert the full dose in one go. Over the loudspeakers that were set up around the property, Sage's voice rang out calmly.

'We are in the process of placing tear gas into the building in an effort to direct you out of the building. This is not an assault. Do not fire your weapons. If you fire, fire will be returned. Do not shoot. This is not an assault. The gas you smell and will continue to detect is a non-lethal tear gas.'

They repeated the message over and over again, but the Davidians continued to fire and the FBI fired back as two of their tanks battered into the building's outer structure and inserted the CS gas. Within the compound, the adults were wearing gas masks but they did not have masks that were suitable for the children, which resulted in them suffering horribly from the irritating fumes. As the tanks continued their assault, the children were led into the vault, a concrete room in the centre of the wood-structured compound. Over an hour later, a chilling conversation between several Davidians was picked up by the listening device.

Unknown male: 'Got some fuel around here?'
Unknown male: 'Right here.'
Unknown male: 'Did you pour it yet?'
Unknown male: 'I haven't yet.'
Unknown male: 'David said pour it, right?'
Unknown male: 'Did he? Do you want it poured?'
Unknown male: 'Come on. Let's pour it.'
Unknown male: 'We want some fuel.'
Unknown male: 'I've got some here.'
Unknown male: 'We should get more hay in here.'
Unknown male: 'I know.'

Just moments later, the FBI saw a wisp of smoke emerge from the second-storey window of the compound and, seconds later, smoke began to rise from two other areas of the ranch. With a fierce wind blowing outside, the fire spread through the wooden structure at an incredible speed, made even worse by the kerosene lamps that were present in almost every room and the thick bales of straw in front of the windows that served as makeshift barricades. Before anything could be done, the whole compound was engulfed in flames. Sage tried to plead with Koresh one last time, begging him to save his people.

'You claim to be the leader. You claim to be the prophet. You claim to be the messiah. Now is the time to lead your people out.'

But his desperate attempts to salvage the situation were in vain. Trapped in the inferno, the Davidians did not even attempt to leave.

As the fire raged, nine cult members were able to escape, but the remaining seventy-six souls all perished in the flames. Fifty-seven adults and seventeen children, including all of Koresh's offspring, were found dead in the remains of the fire. Some had been shot and others had died of suffocation or smoke inhalation. When they found Koresh's body, they confirmed that he had been shot in the head, most likely by his devoted lieutenant, Steve Schneider, who went on to shoot himself.

In the weeks of investigation that followed, over a hundred firearms were recovered from the scene along with 400 rounds of ammunition. Davidian survivors claimed that these items were meant to be sold, but there is no evidence to support that. In the years that followed, nine survivors were taken to court and were convicted of voluntary manslaughter.

After the tragedy, increasing numbers of conspiracy theories began to emerge. Each one was more elaborate and appeared to contain new evidence that would prove that the entire tragedy was in fact a premeditated coup by the ATF and the FBI to eliminate Koresh and his followers. Other, more level-headed apologists claimed that, whilst they did not believe the FBI intended to kill the Davidians, both they and the ATF had made significant errors that led to their deaths and were now involved in a major cover-up to hide the truth. Conflicting theories were based on evidence that was later found. As the Davidians had been deprived of electricity, they were using kerosene lamps, which led apologists to claim that the FBI intentionally or accidentally lit the fire by knocking them over with CS gas canisters that were fired into the building. This is highly improbable as, firstly, they ceased firing CS gas over an hour before the fire began and, secondly, all three fires broke out at the same time, which makes it difficult to believe that it was an accident.

After a detailed investigation by forensic experts, they uncovered evidence which suggested that the fire was caused by arson within the building. If we take into account the information above, combined with photographic evidence and the recording picked up by the listening device, it is very difficult to blame anyone other than the Davidians for causing the fire. One question remains, however. Could the FBI have done more to save those trapped in the fire?

I believe errors were made by the FBI and that the root cause was the poor communication between the negotiators, who were trained to find a peaceful resolution in escalating situations, and the FBI tactical team, who were trained to use extreme force in life-threatening situations. The contrasting combination of the two is meant to be a winning combination, with the tactical team present as a last resort, while the negotiators are there to calm the situation and attempt to find a peaceful resolution. But, at Waco, the sync was off. The tactical team, who had been forced to wait outside at the mercy of the elements for weeks, resented the negotiators for allowing the siege to carry on for so long. They must have thought of their colleagues as feeble social workers, all smug in their warm unit, wasting time and achieving nothing. They were convinced that Koresh would not give in of his own accord, but believed that they could put a swift end to the siege using an aggressive approach. The negotiators, however, having been in communication with Koresh for such a long period, were certain they had the ability to convince the cult prophet to bring an end to the situation.

You may think at this point that Koresh may have been confused, not knowing whether to trust the negotiators or take aggressive action against a potential assault. But the evidence suggests that he played both sides like a master fiddler, who had American authorities playing to his tune.

Koresh was far from innocent. He had many opportunities to bring a peaceful end to the siege. His arrogance and obsession with control prevented him from sending his people out of the building and he is predominantly responsible for the deaths of his followers, particularly if we take into account the recordings that appear to implicate him as the person who ordered the fires to be lit. But the intentions behind his instruction to light the fire do have to be considered. Did he intentionally set out to engulf his community in flames and take them all to their deaths? Or was it an attempt to hold off the tanks? Did he perhaps think that he was giving orders for a clever defensive move, without realising that the strong wind outside, combined with the bales of hay and the compound's wooden structure, would cause an inferno that would spread like wildfire and engulf them all?

Out of the seventy-six that died, twenty were killed by gunshot. It is not known whether they shot themselves or were killed by another Davidian, but it does leave room for doubt as to whether those victims remained in the compound voluntarily until the end.

There are many devoted Davidians who maintain Koresh's innocence to this day, including the majority of the survivors who, despite some having lost their own children and suffered atrocious injury in the fire, continue to remain loyal to their deceased leader. They are steadfast in their belief that he was the messiah and that he will return to fulfil his prophesy one day.

The whole truth of what happened in that building throughout that fateful day will never be known. In my opinion, there is no chance that Koresh would have left the Mount Carmel Center alive, but there is no way of knowing whether matters would have turned out differently had the FBI given the situation more time to develop. Ultimately, however, this tragedy should not be remembered for one proud and delusional man, nor for the blind loyalty of his followers; it should be remembered for the innocent children and infants who were caught up in this fanatical religious statement. They are the true victims of Waco.

CHAPTER 11

Aum Shinrikyo:
Shoko Asahara

Born Chizuo Matsumoto on 2 March 1955 in southern Japan, Asahara was the fourth child in a poor family that lived in a shack. His parents could hardly make ends meet and relied on their skills as tatami mat-makers in order to earn a living. To add to their troubles, Asahara was born with infantile glaucoma, which caused him to go blind in his left eye and left him with partial sight in his right eye at a very young age.

His parents sent him to a school for the blind, where he used his partial sight to his advantage as he was surrounded by fully blind classmates. He dominated and bullied his peers until he was feared by them all and he formed a group of followers who were keen to be under his protection, even if it meant giving him their pocket money in exchange. As a young child he was obsessed with becoming rich, and he carefully saved each coin he extorted from his fellow students until he had quite a respectable amount put aside. He was also an avid sci-fi fan and boasted to his peers that he would one day rule a robot kingdom.

Asahara graduated from school with good grades and a black belt in Judo, but he was hungry for more and wanted nothing else but to enter into politics. He had dreams of becoming the Prime Minister of Japan one day and he studied hard to obtain a place in the prestigious Tokyo University. Despite his hard work, however, he was refused entry. Dejected and humiliated, he was forced to return to his hometown.

Due to his poor sight he did not have many options for his future career, but he chose to study acupuncture and traditional Chinese medicine. He married Tomoko at the age of twenty-three and they went on to have a child. Tomoko was a clever college student and, recognising the drive in her husband, she persuaded her family to fund the opening of a clinic for them to run.

The clinic was a surprising success, but their reputation was damaged when police discovered that Asahara was cheating his clients by selling them fake potions and cures. He was made to pay a small fine, but it was insignificant in comparison to the profit that he had already earned from his scam. His business soon picked up again and, before long, he was earning a respectable living for his family. Yet, he was not satisfied. He wanted a greater purpose and spiritual experiences that would blow his mind away. In a bid to achieve a higher level of spiritual satisfaction, he began practising bizarre rituals and spent long hours, and even days, in a deep state of meditation. Soon, he began to realise that his spirituality and reputation as a healer combined could take him to another level of success and wealth, and he set about making it happen.

He could not have picked a better moment. A wave of religious freedom was washing through Japan in the 1980s and there was an entire generation of young adults that were increasingly drawn to new spiritual movements in their search for enlightenment. Asahara believed more than ever that he had a special purpose, a unique spiritual gift that he had to share with those around him. He heard about one group, Agonshu, who had a modern take on Buddhism and, in 1981 he decided to begin the difficult initiation process to join them. This initiation was physically and spiritually intense, with a thousand days of meditation and other intense rituals. He forged on through it but, once he had completed it, he no longer wanted to join them and he branched out to form his own cult.

In 1984, he registered his company as the Aum Association of Mountain Wizards and appointed himself as chief yoga instructor, using a photograph of himself in levitation as part of his marketing. The photograph, which was later proved to be a fake, drew in hundreds of new members which allowed him to open more schools across the country. With the size of his cult increasing, he set up a leadership team so that he could leave them in charge while he went away on spiritual retreats to meditate and return with fresh doctrines for his followers. On such trips he often met other spiritual minds and stole ideas from them, which he adapted for his own use. When one man in particular spoke to him about his view that Armageddon was imminent, Asahara interpreted this as his calling. When he returned to his group, he revealed to them that he alone had been chosen to save the world by re-organising it with their help.

With his great mission now out in the open, he began to change his image to suit it. He wore long robes, let his hair grow, and instructed his followers to refer to him by his new name, Shoko Asahara. He began giving daily lectures to his members, reiterating his self-appointed mission and ensuring that his position as their leader was steadfast. With increasing members came increasing revenue, which allowed him to travel abroad to spread his doctrines and form alliances with other religious groups. On one such trip in 1987, he met the Dalai Lama and had the opportunity to have his photo taken with him. He brought this back to his flock as proof that he had received a personal blessing; he then went beyond that by falsely claiming that the Dalai Lama had appointed him to enlighten the Japanese population with the true meaning of Buddha's teachings.

It was after this that he wrote his first book, *Secrets of Developing your Spiritual Powers*, in which he claimed to possess the ability to predict the future, read minds and see with x-ray vision. Incredibly, this self-advertising book sold well, which earned him even more members who were willing to pay enormous amounts of money to hear him speak or to have him lay his hands on them. Many fervent followers claimed that he had cured them of serious illnesses, or that they'd had incredible spiritual experiences when he touched them, further enhancing his reputation as a healer amongst his flock.

Soon after, he went on to change the name of his cult to Aum Shinrikyo, meaning Supreme Truth. His movement was now spreading worldwide and his bank balance was thriving, as all his followers were made to pay for the spiritual knowledge that they received. He wanted the cult's name to reflect its blossoming status as a powerful and fresh new religion, and those words fit the bill. His doctrines changed from being predominantly based on Buddhism, to a complex mix of Buddhism, Hinduism and Christianity, with his own interpretations of yoga and a disturbing obsession with the apocalypse. Having studied the Book of Revelation and the prophecies of Nostradamus, a sixteenth-century French astrologer who predicted the end of the world, he had developed his message of doom to such a point that it became the key doctrine in his teachings. He announced that the end of the world as they knew it would take place in 2003, following a nuclear Armageddon, and that only those who achieved the highest levels of enlightenment through his teachings would be saved.

This only made more people want to join his group out of fear for their souls, and his status swiftly changed from that of a guru to that of a messiah. Young and old, rich and poor, educated and ignorant, all flocked to him in their hundreds, prepared to do anything and pay whatever it took to avoid the fast approaching end of the world. Some paid millions to be blessed or taught privately by Asahara; others participated in increasingly crazy rituals such as drinking his blood, or tea made from his beard clippings or his bath water, all in exchange for a large donation to his cult.

By 1988, they had over 1,500 members in Japan alone and an international office in New York. With their finances booming, they built a compound at the base of Mount Fuji. Amidst the beautiful countryside, their compound was rather unattractive; a collection of trailers, shacks and buildings were surrounded by a high security fence which concealed the intense training sessions that were taking place inside. Asahara already had thousands of members, but he wanted to turn a portion of them into his elite squad, comprising the most dedicated followers who would obey his commands without a second thought.

His growing paranoia prompted this move to their new location as he began to see conspiracies everywhere he turned. The British Royal Family, the Freemasons, the Jews and other Japanese religious groups were among those he believed were against the movement that he had created. He needed to form an army of fearless followers who would stop at nothing to maintain their cause and, more importantly, his position.

In order to filter out his most ardent disciples, he put his followers through highly intensive retreats, charging them a small fortune to attend. During these retreats, members were made to sleep on the floor and were allowed only two hours of rest each night, with just one meal given to them during the day. They were told that they had to cut ties with family and friends who were not followers of Aum, and give all their money and assets to the cult. Those who did were welcomed into his inner circle after a service in which they made the oath, 'I entrust my spiritual and physical self and all assets to Aum'.

Those who joined with their children had to sign a disturbing document that prevented them from taking any action against the cult, should their children come to harm. Many families were torn apart as spouses were forced to give their partner up for the cult and children within were allowed no contact with their parent if they were not a member.

Soon, the once welcoming cult became reclusive as those within its inner circle retreated into their hidden world. Behind closed doors, members were increasingly oppressed and handed out harsh punishments for minor transgressions such as voicing doubt or not paying enough attention in lectures. Such actions were punished by being locked away for days in a room with only the voice of Asahara's recordings for company or, worse yet, being deprived of food or sleep for long periods. This did not go entirely unnoticed by the public. Some family members of those trapped in the cult were concerned about the welfare of their loved ones and they contacted the media, which resulted in several articles being published in the press. One newspaper published a series of articles that criticised Asahara's doctrines, which infuriated the cult leader no end. He stormed into their office and demanded that they retract the articles. The newspaper editor, Maki, refused to do so, which resulted in he and his family being subjected to a long hate campaign by the Aum. Cult members spread vicious lies about his loved ones and harassed them twenty-four hours a day by ringing their house 'phone constantly and following them when they left their property. Maki eventually had a stroke, which killed him, and his death was hailed by Asahara as 'heaven's vengeance'.

Around this period, Asahara realised that, among his devoted followers, there were those who possessed skills that were not being put to use for his cause.

Hideo Murai was one of them. Behind a quiet and reserved personality was an extremely intelligent man who had left his promising career as an astrophysicist to join the cult. Asahara recognised his abilities and began to work with him to create the Perfect Salvation Initiation cap, which generated a significant amount of money for the cult. It was a hat that was made out of cloth with a web of miniscule electrodes that sent electronic bursts of energy into the scalp of the person wearing it. They told cult members that the hat would connect them to Asahara's brain waves and synchronise them with his power and energy. The Astral Teleporter came next. Gullible cult members were told that it recorded the vibrations of Asahara's meditation mat, and then sent his vibes to their own through a system of wires. These pulsations were meant to cleanse their astral dimensions and bring them closer to enlightenment.

As his followers were being distracted by these flashy inventions, Asahara secretly put together a team of scientists, who he knew were immensely devoted to him. He instructed them to begin working on the creation of toxins in secret laboratories, located at the cult's headquarters at Mount Fuji. But behind this show of science and spirituality lay misery and fear for certain members of the cult, who were beginning to lose faith. In 1989, one young man in particular had begun to doubt the guru and voiced his concerns about their living conditions to a colleague. When Asahara learnt of this, he called the man into his private chambers and explained that he must be mentally ill if he was thinking of leaving the cult. He diagnosed him with having too much heat within his skull and he ordered his assistants to dunk the young man's head into freezing cold water repeatedly in order to cure his disease. The innocent man died of hypothermia shortly after, his punishment for daring to voice an opinion.

The victim's friend, Shuji Taguchi, was very upset when he heard news of his death and voiced his anger to other cult members. When Asahara found out, Taguchi was dragged to a small cell where he was bound with ropes and questioned for hours. Exhausted and angry, he blurted out his feelings of resentment towards Asahara, telling his captors that he lost trust in him as a leader. Hearing of his confession, the cult leader told his men that Taguchi could not stay at the compound as he would poison the minds of his other followers; but he added that he could not leave either, as he would most likely report them to police. He told them to give the young man one last chance to repent and left them with the instruction, 'If he refuses, you know what you must do'.

Having been given the ultimatum, Taguchi remain steadfast and demanded that they let him go. It was this request that sealed his fate. Four of Asahara's men held him down while another attempted to strangle him with a rope. Taguchi fought back but, eventually, one of his assailants broke his neck, killing him instantly. They doused his body in gasoline and burnt it in a drum, dumping his ashes in nearby shrubbery. Months later, when his family rang to speak to him, they were told that he was unable to get to the 'phone. They waited several months before attempting to contact him again, unsuccessfully. They reported him missing, but authorities were unable to find any proof of foul play and the case went cold. This was enough to spark even greater concern amongst the families of other cult members.

One family in particular grew tired of the police's refusal to help them in their quest to free their underage daughter from Aum and they sought the help of Tsutsumi Sakamoto, a lawyer from Yokohama, who was reputed for his work as a human rights' advocate. Soon, more families came forward and, by the end of 1989, Sakamoto was handling twenty-three separate cases against Aum Shinrikyo. Some of his cases involved the parents of under-aged children who were trapped in Aum communities. Others were taken out by concerned relatives who believed that their loved ones were being held against their will by the cult. He also took on the cases of several ex-members who were suing the movement in an attempt to recuperate the money they had paid for bogus treatments and medicine. Sakamoto was a fierce lawyer who had experience with cults having previously taken on another case against the Moonies. His wife, Satoko, was equally as passionate about assisting those who were oppressed and despite having a young toddler at home, she dedicated much of her time to working with her husband on the case.

Asahara had his own legal team led by Aoyama, a twenty-nine-year-old lawyer, who was very ambitious and, more importantly, a dedicated follower of Aum. He tried to appease the situation by offering to mediate a meeting between ex-members and their relatives that were still in the cult. But Sakamoto was not fooled by this effort to divert him from what he wanted to achieve. He demanded that Asahara release all the underage children in the cult. He also brought the legal proceedings to the media's attention, exposing the cult's oppression of its members and fraudulent activities. Asahara responded in the same manner as he had done with Maki. He arranged a campaign of harassment against the lawyer. His followers distributed leaflets in cities across Japan in an attempt to discredit Sakamoto; they also rang his office and home at all hours of day and night, leaving threatening messages in a bid to deter him from moving forward with the case.

Sakamoto was not a man to take things lying down and he upped his legal war against the cult, requesting that they provide proof that Asahara's blood really did contain a special power. He knew that, with that request, he would have them cornered. If they did not comply, they would be seen to be hiding something; if they allowed an outside laboratory to test his blood, their entire operation would be proved to be a sham and they would have to refund thousands of people that they had conned. Asahara was furious and he knew that he had to silence this outspoken lawyer. He called his most loyal men together and they formed a plan to get rid of him. His scientists had been testing various drugs and poisons and they had concocted a mixture that could kill a man almost instantly.

The following day, on 3 November 1989, they carried out their plan. Cult members Murai, martial arts master Hashimoto and physician Dr Tomomasa Nakagawa were among the small group that set out to execute it. Their plan was to kidnap Sakamoto on his way home from work but after waiting for several hours at Shinkansen train station, they realised to their dismay that it was 'Culture Day', a national holiday in Japan, and therefore Sakamoto would not have gone to work that day. Asahara instructed a change of plan; they were to carry out the assassination at his apartment instead.

Following their new orders, the men waited until 3 a.m. and then broke into Sakamoto's family home. They attacked Sakamoto as he slept, bashing him in the head with a hammer. His wife, Satoko, woke up and began to scream; she, too, was beaten until she could no longer fight back and they finished her off by strangling her to death. They injected both with the poison but, incredibly, Sakamoto continued to struggle until they put him out of his misery by strangling him. Then, they did the unthinkable. Dr Nakagawa bent over the crib of the sleeping child and injected him with a lethal dose of poison. They smashed the teeth of both parents, in order to make it more difficult for them to be identified. Then, they crammed the bodies into metal drums which they hid in three separate locations, far from the cult's compound. When they returned to their master, he congratulated them on their work and rewarded them financially.

When the lawyer failed to turn up at his office the following week, family members travelled to his house, where they were perplexed to find an intact, yet empty house. Nothing had been moved or taken apart from the bed sheets which, unbeknownst to them, had been burned by the killers. To the family, it appeared that Sakamoto had simply vanished with his wife and child, but then they found something that caused them great concern. On the floor, near a closet, lay a badge that had the symbol of Aum inscribed on it. Worried, they informed local police, but they were ignored. The authorities believed that Sakamoto had vanished voluntarily with the intent to create a media storm against the Aum cult. But when his disappearance hit the news, it captivated the public's interest and, a few weeks later, the police begrudgingly asked Asahara to come in for an interview. The cult leader conveniently fled to Germany, with the excuse that he had to oversee work in one of his branches there. When he returned to Japan, he arranged a press conference and vehemently denied all involvement, claiming that thousands of identical badges had been distributed. The authorities looked into his claim and confirmed the truth of it. They had no way to prove that the badge was placed there by a member of Aum and, with no further evidence, the case eventually went cold.

Filled with confidence, Asahara felt that there were no limits to what he could achieve, or to what he could get away with. His political ambitions resurfaced and he decided to run for the national parliamentary elections in 1990. He entered several of his followers into the elections as well, hoping that at least a few of them would obtain seats in the Lower House. Their methods of campaigning were very unusual. Wearing masks of Asahara's face, they sang and danced in the streets, mixing political promises with religious speeches that warned of an impending apocalypse. They also used bribes and threats to persuade voters to side with them. That was not enough, however, and Asahara suffered a crushing blow to his pride when he lost the elections, with not one of his members gaining a seat in the Lower House. Worse yet, the electoral campaign had attracted quite a large amount of public attention and the media was now watching them closer than ever before, waiting for them to make a wrong move.

The cult tyrant was furious. He had been humiliated through his recent defeat and was more paranoid and bitter than ever. He wanted someone to pay and he began to preach an even more radical message to his followers. No longer would they await the apocalypse; their mission was now to get it started. He told his followers they were to raise an army, stockpile weapons and train for an upcoming war. Again, he turned to his greatest assets, his scientists and other highly skilled members of his flock. Murai became the brains behind a new project, assisted by Seiichi Endo, a genetics engineer who specialised in molecular biology. Together, they created one of the most deadly poisons that exists, Clostridium Botulinum.

Asahara moved his closest followers to a retreat on the island of Okinawa, while his hit team sprayed the poison in central Tokyo, targeting areas near Japanese parliament buildings. Their goal was to assassinate key members of the Japanese government, with the view that their deaths would enable their messiah, Asahara, to take control. However, for some reason, the poison did not work and no damage was done. Asahara ordered his scientists to continue working on alternative chemicals and, in order to deflect attention he travelled to Moscow where his group of followers had been growing steadily for the last few months.

Using clever marketing and hefty bribes to local officials, Asahara soon became a respected and welcome figure in Russia. The size of his following grew immensely and, by early 1992, he had over 10,000 members, including government officials. But that was not the primary reason he was there. During his trip, he bribed key military and national security officials who, in exchange for large sums of money, allowed Asahara's engineer, Kiyohide Hayakawa, to glean information on chemical and nuclear weapons. When Asahara left Russia, he left Hayakawa behind, ordering him to learn as much as he could and to set up contacts and black market supply lines for weapons and illegal chemicals.

By 1993, their plans were steadily in place. This time, the cult's scientists were working on a new chemical weapon, sarin gas. This lethal gas does not have odour or colour which makes it almost impossible for its victims to protect themselves from it. It is a nerve agent that attacks the nervous system and can kill its victim within a minute, even at low dosage. Usually, death is caused by asphyxia, as the victim is gradually unable to breathe due to loss of control over their breathing muscles. Victims will usually suffer convulsions and violent vomiting followed by the inability to control their bodily functions and, finally, death. As the scientists worked on the gas, Hayakawa was ordered to oversee the production of military weapons in the form of explosives, guns and tanks with the aim to provide weapons for over a thousand of his followers by 1995. They built a new warehouse on their compound near Mount Fuji, where the production took place. Asahara also instructed former military men within his cult to train his followers in military tactics; they then formed an elite troop of the most skilled soldiers to protect their leader and participate in upcoming assaults.

Financially, the cult was booming. They opened a chain of IT stores when the market was flourishing and they purchased companies and properties all over Japan. Recruitment was still going strong, which provided the group with a steady and large flow of money each month from members alone. It is said that, at this point, Asahara's net worth was in excess of one billion dollars and he lived a life of luxury, very much in contrast to the grim conditions his followers were forced to live in.

In June 1993, Asahara ordered another attack. As the sarin gas was not yet perfected, they decided to use a strain of the botulism virus that scientist Endo believed he had successfully produced. The royal wedding of Prince Naruhito was taking place that month, which gave them the perfect opportunity to take out the Japanese royal family and government officials in one hit. They spread the virus throughout the city but, again, the product failed to deliver. Further unsuccessful attempts followed. In one experiment, they used anthrax which apart from producing a foul smell and causing stomach upsets, produced no harmful results. They realised later that the strain they were using was not a virulent strain.

Frustrated with the length of time it was taking to produce results, Asahara sent teams of experts to various countries worldwide to study chemical and biological weapons, hoping to find one that they could reproduce successfully. He also continued his efforts to buy nuclear warheads and other, more destructive weaponry on the black market, but with little success. Just when he thought that he would never achieve his dream, there was a breakthrough at the lab. Masami Tsuchiya, a chemist working with Endo, finally managed to produce liquid sarin in October 1993. After over 15 million dollars had been spent on chemical production, Asahara was estatic. But, with so many failed attempts behind them, he wanted to have the product thoroughly tested before they used it, and he knew the perfect place to do just that. Earlier that year, he had purchased a remote sheep ranch in the Western Australian outback, which was ideal for experiments.

The cult leader and his closest lieutenants travelled to the ranch where they tested the sarin on a herd of sheep. It is not known how they managed to smuggle the chemical into the country, but somehow they found a way and the experiment was a success. Thirty sheep were killed after being exposed to the poisonous substance and Asahara was overjoyed. He was now ready to strike. However, before he executed his plan, he wanted to do one final test, this time on humans beings.

A few months prior, Asahara had attempted to purchase a company located a couple of hours from Tokyo in the town of Matsumoto; however, the owner, upon discovering that his client was a cult leader, put in a legal motion to cancel the sale. The court case was reaching its end and the three judges involved had retired to consider their verdict. The cult leader knew he stood very little chance of winning the case and he decided that the three judges would be the perfect targets for his final test.

On 27 June 1994, he sent his assault team to carry out the attack, with a truck filled with sarin. Late that night, they drove through a residential area where the judges were known to be staying and released the gas, with no thought for the hundreds of innocents who lived in the surrounding houses of the neighbourhood. The gas seeped through the air through an atomiser but, in a twist of fate, the wind suddenly changed direction and, instead of the gas blowing in the direction of the judges' dormitory, it blew into the houses nearby, killing and harming the animals and residents within. Eight innocent people died that night and over 200 were injured. The incident sparked a large-scale police investigation, during which an anonymous tip-off was sent to police. It pointed the finger at Aum and hinted that there would be an attack of a larger scale in the near future. Astonishingly, no action was taken against the cult.

Asahara was pleased with the outcome of the attack. After all, if the gas had produced such good results in an open-air environment, then it would cause devastation in a contained area. Although he knew that he had escaped punishment for yet another crime, he also knew that his good luck could not last forever. Over the following months, he became extremely paranoid and unleashed his fury on anyone who he believed was attempting to get in the way of his plan to overthrow the government. One elderly cult member, who had given her lifesavings to the cult, became disillusioned and escaped the commune, going into hiding for her own safety. When Asahara's men were unable to find her, he sent his mercenary, Yashihiro Inoue, to track her down. Failing to do so, Inoue kidnapped the woman's sixty-eight-year-old brother, Kiyoshi Kariya, and brought him to the Mount Fuji compound. There he was beaten, drugged and tortured for hours, but he refused to give up his sister's location and he died protecting his sibling. His body was cooked in an industrial microwave for two days before being left to dissolve in nitric acid.

This courageous man had the foresight to leave behind a note after receiving a strange 'phone call a few hours before his abduction. The caller was enquiring about his sister's whereabouts and Kariya, knowing her situation, hid a note in his house which read, 'If I disappear, I was abducted by Aum Shinrikyo'. The police had no choice but to act upon this information and they began to work on a plan to raid the Aum compound.

But Asahara was just as busy making his own plans and ensuring that his men were ready to carry them out. Their goal was to launch a sarin gas attack in the subways of Tokyo in order to cause as much chaos and death as they possibly could. According to the narcissistic cult leader, this attack would throw the country into chaos and would spark tensions between Japan and the United States as the Japanese government would blame them for the attack and vice versa. Then, other world powers would get involved resulting in a Third World War, the Armageddon that Asahara had predicted for so long. In his mind, all of this would end with him taking control of the government and declaring himself Emperor of Japan.

During peak rush hour on 20 March 1995, they carried out their murderous task. Five subway trains across Tokyo were targeted to be gassed as they approached Kasumigaseki, one of the busiest stations in the capital. The five men who would deposit the gas were physics graduate Kenichi Hirose, artificial intelligence graduate Yasuo Hayashi, senior heart specialist Dr Ikuo Hayashi and applied physics graduates Toru Toyoda and Masato Yokoyama. The scientists prepared bags for them, stuffed with the lethal liquid poison. They gave each man an umbrella with a sharpened tip, which they were to use to pierce the bags before leaving their trains. This would allow the gas to spread throughout the carriages once they had made their escape. They also carried antidote pills, just in case they were accidentally exposed to the gas.

The plan worked. As each train grew closer to Kasumigaseki station, the five men punctured the bags and left the train. The gas began to leak and the effects were instantaneous. By the time each train pulled into the next station, commuters were stumbling off its carriages, vomiting and coughing while others collapse onto the platform floor, convulsing as they suffocated helplessly. Within just a few hours there were more than a thousand injured victims, fifty of which suffered severe injuries caused by the sarin nerve agent. Twelve innocent people died that day.

Police were baffled. Fearing that the city was under attack, the army was called in while emergency services frantically tried to cope with the injured commuters. Meanwhile, as some lay dying, the five terrorists returned to the compound where they were praised and financially rewarded for their bravery and the success of their mission. They were then sent to safe houses, where they were instructed to hide until further notice.

By early afternoon, military specialists had identified the substance as sarin gas. It was a revelation that sparked a wave of panic across the city as residents tried to protect themselves against another attack. Despite having no hard evidence that the Aum were involved, Tokyo police decided to move forward with the pre-planned raids on Aum properties, based on their initial concern that they were involved in Kariya's disappearance. But each time they raided a location, the Aum community living there appeared to have been tipped off. It became clear that there was a mole in the police department, but they had no choice but to continue and hope that some evidence would be found.

Warned of an upcoming raid, the compound at Mount Fuji burst into a flurry of activity as they desperately tried to get rid of evidence and vacate the premises before the authorities arrived. Incriminating equipment and chemical supplies were hidden or destroyed and Asahara went into hiding. With access to millions of dollars, it was not difficult for him to disappear.

On 22 March, just two days after the attack in Tokyo, over a thousand police officers raided the compound. Armed with assault weapons and chemical suits, they barged their way through the gates and stormed through each building, arresting the few Aum members that were still there, destroying the evidence. What they found shocked officials at the highest levels of government and sent a chill through the spines of the Japanese population. Over 200 types of chemicals were discovered onsite along with the equipment necessary to transform them into lethal weapons. Despite the cult's efforts to destroy the chemicals, there was still a large enough quantity onsite to kill a third of the population of Tokyo. They also found a military helicopter and millions of dollars' worth in gold and cash hidden in a safe.

Asahara denied all involvement in the attack via a video message to police, claiming that the US was behind it and were pinning the blame on the cult in order to get away with it. But the police would not be fooled this time. After their discovery at Mount Fuji, they were more determined than ever to hunt down this terrorist leader and his minions. Over the next month, key members of his leadership team were taken into custody, including Kiyohide Hayakawa and Dr Ikuo Hayashi. In retaliation, Asahara issued a statement, warning the public that a major disaster would occur on 15 April. The entire country went into high alert as authorities prepared for another terrorist strike.

Governments and experts across the globe were baffled at the severity of this situation. What, at first had appeared to be a New Age, peaceful religious movement had turned into a violent terrorist cult that seemed hell bent on causing a global war. Many countries went into high alert, particularly the US, where the cult had a significant number of followers.

As dawn broke on the 15 April 1995, the country braced itself for the worst. Hospitals had stocked up on antidotes to be administered in the event of another chemical attack. Offices and shops shut for the day and many fled the city in the hope that the rural countryside would not be targeted. The day crawled by in slow motion and relief could be felt everywhere when nothing out of the ordinary occurred.

Police now had solid evidence that the cult had produced sarin gas and further raids and arrests were made. Masami Tsuchiya and Seiichi Endo were discovered in a basement at the Mount Fuji compound, which had been missed in the initial raid. Their senior scientist Hideo Murai was stabbed to death by a stranger as he tried to make his way into an Aum building; his murderer said that he acted out in rage, horrified over the deaths caused by the gas attack.

On 5 May, another attack was foiled, this time at Shinjuku station in Tokyo, which was exceptionally busy that day due to it being a public holiday. The bag containing the chemicals was found and contained just in time, with police realising that, had it not been, over 20,000 people were likely to have been killed. Yoshiro Inoue was arrested a few days later and, on 16 May, Asahara was finally captured, having been found hiding in one of the buildings on the Mount Fiji compound. He must have believed that this would be the last place that they would look for him, as the property had previously been searched on several occasions. But he was wrong and, for the Japanese population, the nightmare was finally over. Or was it?

Police were on high alert for several months following Asahara's arrest, and they were right to be concerned. Over the next few weeks, further incidents occurred. A parcel was sent to the governor of Tokyo, which contained a bomb that detonated in the hands of his secretary, who unfortunately lost several fingers. Four cyanide devices were found in various subway stations, but luckily, they malfunctioned, which spared the lives of thousands of people.

In 1996, Asahara was brought to trial facing twenty-seven counts of murder. Seventeen charges were brought against him and the cult leader pleaded not guilty to all charges. The media quickly named it 'the trial of the century' due to the worldwide interest in the case. Asahara had a large team of lawyers working on his defence, which initially rested on his claim that his leadership team had planned and carried out the attacks without his knowledge or consent. It must have been a terrible blow to his closest followers to have discovered that he was now betraying them in a bid to save his own life. Some went on to testify against him, but many remained unwaveringly loyal and protested his innocence.

As details emerged in the trial, the public were shocked to learn that these horrific attacks and murders were not the work of some city gang but that of a team of masterminds. A large number of the men and women who were involved were highly intelligent people, some of whom had brilliant careers and social standing. In a country that values high education and cultural etiquette, it was horrifying to be faced with the reality that evil could be found in the most intelligent of minds and the most pleasant of faces.

At the start, Asahara was rather cooperative with his defence team but, mid-trial, he made the decision to resign from his position as the leader of Aum, in order to prevent the cult from being forced to shut down. Once that decision had been made, he retreated into silence and did not speak another word in court, preferring to sit in the dock with his eyes closed for the majority of the time, occasionally mumbling incoherently as if he were in a trance.

The law eventually caught up with this cold-hearted fanatic and he was found guilty of thirteen out of the seventeen charges, including the Sakamoto family murders. He was sentenced to death by hanging on 27 February 2004. Calling the Tokyo attack, 'an unprecedentedly brutal and serious crime', the presiding judge who read out the sentence expressed his disgust that the cult leader had attempted to place the blame on his followers, and that he had failed to apologise to the victims of his crime. It is said the mass murderer yawned and showed no emotion or remorse as his sentence was being handed down. His defence team appealed the decision, claiming that Asahara was mentally unfit; however, following psychiatric examinations, he was found to be behaving strangely out of choice and not due to any mental illnesses. This was made clear when the psychiatrist realised that he was able and willing to speak coherently and regularly broke his silence when he was in his cell. The decision was upheld and he currently awaits execution. In Japan, they do not announce execution dates publically. In June 2012, however, authorities informed the public that the planned date had been postponed due to the arrest of several Aum suspects, who were wanted for their involvement in the terrorist attack in Tokyo. He now awaits death in jail.

Justice was handed down to the five men who had planted the gas on the subway. Dr Hayashi, having cooperated with police upon arrest, was sentenced to life imprisonment. Hirose, Toyoda, Yokoyama and Hayashi were all sentenced to death. Other members of the Aum management team were also sentenced to death, including Endo, Hayakawa, Tsuchiya, Inoue, Dr Nakagawa, Hashimoto and cult executive, Kazuaki Okazaki. Asahara's wife, Tomoko Matsumoto, was arrested and imprisoned for six years for her involvement in the murder of disillusioned Aum member Kotaro Ochida, who was strangled to death in 1994. This victim was just one of many cult members who were killed for wanting to leave the group and whose remains were found at various cult properties during police raids.

Incredibly, the cult continues to operate to this day. After changing their name to Aleph in January 2000, the leadership mantel fell on Aum spokesman Fumihiro Joyu who, in a statement on their website, claimed that they acknowledged Asahara's involvement in the crimes. But he also went on to add that they still consider him to be a genius of meditation and continue to follow his teachings. It is also rumoured that to this day, the cult still think of Asahara as the messiah and are secretly preparing for the apocalypse, which fuels concerns that they may turn violent in the future. The cult, which at one stage had reached membership levels of around 30,000, is now said to have in the region of 2,000 followers, with an estimated 1,800 full-time members. Their finances are still flourishing due to the number of businesses they inherited from Aum and, in recent years, they have reportedly paid out compensation to the victims of Aum crimes. Aleph is not considered a threat to the public, but they are still under a renewable surveillance order, which allows authorities to closely monitor their activities and carry out inspections on all cult communes. All that remains is to hope that the reformed cult has truly purged its ranks of those that consider Asahara's actions to be in any way acceptable.

A news article was published in July 2013 which stated that, on a recent police inspection of the cult's headquarters, a pile of photographs were found featuring various Japanese lawyers, high-ranking public security employees and police officers. A ten-inch knife had been stabbed through the pile. Such a discovery, if true, is highly concerning as it suggests that the cult has only cleaned up its image for the public and that, behind closed doors, they still harbour hatred for the Japanese government. Joyu has since resigned from his post as leader, reportedly over an internal conflict as to whether they should continue to worship Asahara as the messiah. It is unclear who has been running the cult since, but Joyu went on to form his own cult, Hikari no Wa, or The Circle of Rainbow Light, which is also being closely monitored by Japanese authorities. Their mother group, Aum Shinrikyo, is officially considered a terrorist group by various countries and organisations including the US, the European Union and Canada.

Shoko Asahara was a highly manipulative cult leader who used the loyalty of his followers to increase his wealth and attempt to cause a world war for his own political interests. One can only hope that his time in prison awaiting death will give him the opportunity to consider the impact that his actions had on thousands of innocent minds and the families of those whose lives were taken for his own gain.

CHAPTER 12

Order Of The Solar Temple:
Joseph Di Mambro and Luc Jouret

When the fire brigade of Morin Heights Quebec, were called out to a chalet to put out a fire, they assumed that it was a regular residence fire that needed to be attended to. No one, including the firemen and authorities in this touristic skiing town, were prepared for the scene they would discover once they had extinguished the flames.

As they searched through the smoldering debris of what was once a quaint chalet, they came across two incinerated bodies in the living room. The unidentified bodies belonged to a male and female, but they had yet to determine whether they had died accidentally or not. Before they were able to speculate further, they found something else that shocked even the most experienced firefighter to the core. The body of a three-month-old child was found hidden in a closet with an adult male and a similarly aged female. A wooden stake lay across the infant's tiny chest, which had been punctuated with stab wounds.

Baffled by the nature of these gruesome crimes, police began a full-scale investigation to determine what exactly had taken place that night. It would not be long before they confirmed what they had already suspected—that the adults found with the child were his parents and that all three had been brutally murdered. This led to even more questions about the first two bodies that were found, as they did not appear to have suffered the same fate. The autopsies corroborated their initial findings and revealed that the small family had died a few days before the fire consumed the chalet. In what now appeared to be a vicious attack, the father had been stabbed fifty times in the back, and the mother, twelve times in the throat, chest and back. Their child had been knifed six times in the chest and police were still bewildered by the wooden stake. Was this the work of some dark witchcraft society? It would not be long before this heinous crime was linked to a sinister and secretive cult, The Order of the Solar Temple, which was created and run by two very deranged men.

Formally trained as a doctor, Belgian Luc Jouret began to take an interest in alternative medicines in his thirties, notably homeopathy along with other forms of holistic healing. Based in France on the edge of the Swiss border, he obtained certification to practice as a homeopathic physician and, before long he began to develop a fascination with aliens. He gave lectures on alternative medicines and the paranormal across Europe and Eastern Canada and it was during one of these lectures that he met Joseph Di Mambro. Di Mambro was a French jeweller by trade and a member of the Rosicrucian Order, a secretive group that was founded by H. Spencer Lewis. Not long after leaving the group, he was charged with swindling, which prompted him to leave the south of France for a region near the Swiss border. There he worked as a psychologist until his scam was unmasked and he was again charged, but this time for fraudulently posing as a medical professional.

Soon after, he set up his own cult in Geneva, which he named The Golden Way, and he invited Jouret to lecture at one of his conventions. When he heard him speak he was amazed by the younger man's charisma and ability to influence a crowd. He also noticed that they had many beliefs and ideas in common and this prompted him to make an offer to Jouret. By joining forces, they would be the perfect team: one inspirational enough to win over new recruits, the other clever enough to run the show in the background. Jouret could not turn down such a tempting offer and, together, they created their brotherhood in 1984, the Order of the Solar Temple. Such a glamorous name did not appear out of nowhere. It was later discovered that Jouret had been involved with another very secretive cult called the Renewed Order of the Solar Temple, which was run by Julien Origas, a right-wing politician, who was rumoured to have had links to the Nazis during the Second World War. Unsatisfied with the position of follower, Jouret had hoped to branch out and create his own brand of religion. What better way to do so than to join minds with Di Mambro, who had already established a following?

Their doctrines incorporated ideas from various religions with strong influences from Christianity and the ideals of the Knights Templar, which Di Mambro had learnt much about during his time spent within the Rosicrucian Order. They also blended in their strong belief in aliens and the conviction that they were the chosen ones, destined to complete the mission of a pre-existing medieval Order of the Temple, who had not been able to fulfil their destiny. To enhance this illusion, they would perform flamboyant ceremonies complete with medieval robes, swords and other ritual tools. These mystic sessions attracted a number of curious souls who were in search of a meaning to their existence. Once they had assembled a core group of followers, they put them through a strict spiritual programme that included rituals and occult practices, all the while ingraining in them the belief that they would one day play a part in bringing a New Age to the world, to make way for the Second Coming of Christ.

Jouret took ownership of the marketing and recruitment for the movement and he continued to lecture across various countries with the aim of gaining sponsors and disciples. Unlike most cult leaders, he did not target the downtrodden, weak members of society; he aimed higher, actively pursuing the rich and socially or politically powerful figures. His lectures, which were initially focused on alternative medicines and spiritual healing, soon included apocalyptic messages as he increasingly spoke of natural disasters and the eventual demise of the planet due to ecological decline. Meanwhile, Di Mambro ran the cult behind the scenes and exerted immense control over their followers. The core of the cult's leadership was called the Synarchy of the Temple and it was run by thirty-three of the cult's most senior members in a brotherhood called the Elder Brothers of the Rosy Cross. The membership list of this brotherhood was kept a secret from the rest of the cult's population.

As their following grew, they created additional ranks of seniority amongst members, mostly in the hope of gaining further financial donations, as avid followers strived to achieve the next level of spiritual glorification. Di Mambro kept a close eye on the finances of the cult and he ensured that they cashed in on each level, with the most lucrative being the new entries into their core membership group, as members were required to give up all their worldly possessions and salaries in exchange for a place in one of their communal houses. As their group of followers increased, he supervised the opening of additional communes, which they called lodges. Each lodge was run by three elders who reported to a Regional Commander. The spiritual progress of each member was closely monitored as they rose through the preset levels within the order, beginning with The Brothers of Parvis into the The Knights of the Alliance and, finally, The Brothers of the Ancient Times. Whenever a cult member reached a new level, a lavish ceremony would take place in which medieval attire would be worn and the subject would be knighted at the Lodge's altar. At the cult's headquarters, Jouret would often summon spirits at such rituals, which convinced many onlookers to join the cult.

However, as their numbers grew, so did the leaders' power and their ability to control. Their message changed dramatically; the once docile and theatrical occult teachings turned into prophetic tales of doom that consumed both them and their flock. They began to preach of a worldwide famine and war, which would result in a great fire that would consume the planet. The only place where they could survive such a tragedy was Quebec, so for their own safety, the leadership group relocated there amidst the booming growth of their organisation. It was a comfortable relocation. At this point, the organisation had lodges in several countries including Australia, Switzerland, Martinique and France. Their following now included over 400 members of middle and upper class society. Some were key figures of government or local authorities; but, to this day, many were never exposed as being members of the cult. Such wealthy disciples brought great financial gain and the two leaders lived in luxury, which did not go unnoticed by some of their more astute followers.

They attempted to placate them by coming up with a string of intense revelations. Di Mambro was very much in control of the internal spiritual progress of the cult and, despite his acceptance of Jouret as co-leader, he in no way allowed him to interfere with his dominance when it came to internal affairs. Di Mambro now had two children and he was intent on setting up his offspring as the heirs to his throne. To secure their place, he claimed to have received a prophesy that his son, Elie, had been created through a holy union of the Gods. However, more importantly, he claimed that his daughter, Emmanuelle, had been conceived through supernatural conception whilst he and his wife were visiting Israel and, hence, she was destined to be their next leader.

The two men also began to introduce their concept that, one day, they would all leave Earth and transit to Sirius, a distant star that would be their home once they had fulfilled their mission in the physical world. Their tales convinced many. With his daughter now isolated from the public to maintain her purity, Di Mambro went on to claim that he received cosmic messages through her. But that was not enough to blind the more intelligent members of their flock, particularly when they took into account other factors that were rather disturbing, such as unmarried Jouret's recent insistence that he had to have sex prior to rituals in order to muster the strength to summon the spirits. He demanded that any female he desired, married or not, must be willing to service him sexually as and when required. As one can imagine, the majority of his male disciples were very unhappy with this. His co-founder, Di Mambro, also abused his power over female 'knights' within their close circle. He would regularly force them to perform sex acts on him under the threat that he could break up their marriage or relationship, simply by claiming that they and their lover were not cosmically compatible.

Discord erupted when cult members realised that the money they had donated towards cult projects, was in fact funding their leaders' increasingly luxurious lifestyles. Resentment set in and, in the early 1990s, some were no longer prepared to keep silent. A whirlwind of rumours began to circle the communes and, when Jouret was arrested for his involvement in the attempted purchase of firearms and silencers, those rumours only increased and spread further. Although Jouret got away with one year of probation and a fine, his arrest sparked the attention of authorities in Quebec and they began to investigate the illusive cult's practices and, more importantly, their financial accounts. This lead to a newspaper article being published which dealt a harsh blow to the cult's reputation. Di Mambro and Jouret fled Canada shortly after, taking their closest followers back to Switzerland with them.

A significant number of cult members left at this point. With the leaders becoming increasingly controlling and secretive about the cult's finances, many were no longer willing to trust in Jouret and Di Mambro. This would herald the start of a very dark period for the co-founders. After all, with no ecological disasters in sight and their New Age not even close on the horizon, they were destined for only one end. Their group was close to disbandment and even the cult leaders no longer agreed on the same doctrines and principles. Although they argued over the dynamics of their roles within the brotherhood, they appeared to agree on one solution. They knew that the game was over and they arranged for letters to be sent out to their most loyal followers in October 1994, which would bring an explosive end to their fellowship. In these letters, they informed their following that the time had come. The apocalypse was now imminent and their new world on the star Sirius was ready to welcome them. It was time to transit. But, unlike previous messages which depicted the transit in a spiritual sense, this message was very clear as to what method of transition would be used in order to gain access to Sirius. They had to give up their earthly bodies and purify their souls through fire. Only then could they move on to their new life.

The countdown had begun, but the cult leaders had every intention of taking out one particular family before they transitioned. It was a family that, in their eyes, had played a key role in smearing their reputation and who threatened the birth-right of Di Mambro's daughter and heir. Tony Dutoit had recently left the cult and he lived with his wife, Nicki, and their young child, Christopher-Emmanuel, in Morin Heights, Quebec. Tony had previously worked as an electrician for the inner circle of the cult and, during his time on the job, was asked to install mechanical devices in their chapel. He later discovered that they were electronic projection devices that would create holograms during ceremonies; these holograms would deceive the attendees into believing they were seeing spirits that had been conjured by Jouret when, in fact, Di Mambro was operating the devices from a hidden room. Tony also found out that Di Mambro was stealing funds from the cult's accounts and, outraged, he told his colleagues of his findings and exposed the leaders as frauds. His accusations caused a number of families to leave the cult, disgusted that they had been deceived and financially defrauded by their leaders. Tony and Nicki had also committed another crime in the eyes of the cult tyrants. Di Mambro had, in

1 *The Battle between the Israelites and the Amalekites* by Gerard Hoet, 1728.

2 *Victory of Joshua over Amorites* by Nicolas Poussin, 1842.

3 View of the plateau, upon which the city of Masada was built. The Roman ramp can be seen stretching down the right side of the plateau. (*Photograph by Andrew Shiva*)

4 An aerial view of the ruins of Masada city. (Photograph by Andrew Shiva)

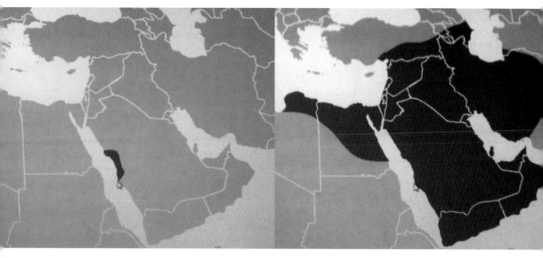

5 *Muslim Territory AD 632 (left) vs AD 643 (right). (Created by M. Adil)*

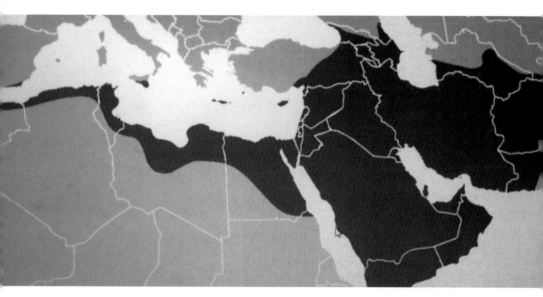

6 Muslim Territory AD 655. (*Created by M. Adil*)

7 *Tomas de Torquemada*,
Unknown Artist.

8 *The Inquisition Tribunal* by Francisco Goya, 1819.

9 *Torture Chamber*, Unknown Artist, Eighteenth Century.

10 *Members of a gang of thugs in the prison of Aurangabad*, Unknown Artist, 1869.

11 *The Goddess Kali* by Raja Ravi Varma, *c.* 1906.

12 Police mug-shots taken of Charles Manson. (*Courtesy of the Ventura County Police Department*)

13 Police mug-shots of Tex Watson and Susan Atkins. (*Courtesy of the California Prison of Corrections and the Los Angeles County Police Department*)

14 Jim Jones receiving a Martin Luther King, Jr. Award from Glide Memorial Church in San Francisco. (*Photograph by Nancy Wong*)

15 Congressman Leo Ryan. (*Courtesy of Office of the Clerk, US House of Representatives*)

16 Adolfo Constanzo.

17 Jeffrey Lundgren is sworn in at his trial. (*Courtesy of © Bettmann/ CORBIS*)

18 Police mugshot of David Koresh. (*Courtesy of McLennan County Sheriff's Office*)

19 Aerial view of the Mount Carmel Centre shortly after the start of the fire. (*Courtesy of the Federal Bureau of Investigation*)

20 Shoko Asahara. (*Courtesy of ©*
STRINGER/epa/CORBIS)

21 A transit worker sits by a victim
of the Tokyo Sarin attack. (*Courtesy
of Noburu Hashimoto/Sygma/*
Corbis)

22 Joseph DiMambro, his wife Jocelyne and their daughter Emmanuelle. (*Courtesy of © Stephane Ruet/Sigma/ CORBIS*)

23 Luc Jouret. (*Courtesy of AFP/Getty Images*)

24 Marshall Applewhite and Bonnie Nettles. (*Courtesy of* © *Bettmann/CORBIS*)

25 Hale Bopp Comet. (*Photograph by E. Kolmhofer and H. Raab at the Johannes Kepler Observatory, Austria*)

26 Joseph Kibweteere and his estranged wife Theresa. (*Courtesy of © Reuters/CORBIS*)

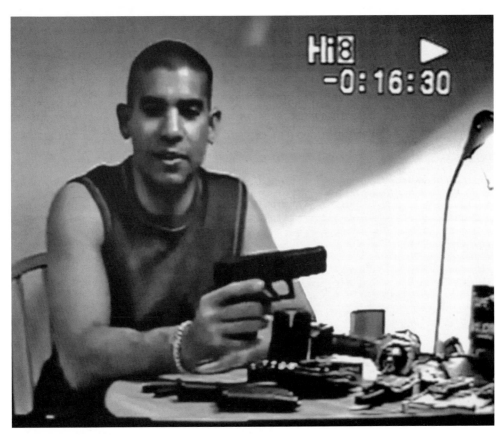

27 Ricky Rodriguez in the self-recorded home video that he left behind.

the past few years, begun to control further aspects of his members' personal lives, including their right to have children. He specifically forbade the Dutoits to conceive a child after Nicki suffered a miscarriage but, in a show of defiance, she fell pregnant again shortly after and gave birth to a baby boy.

Furious, Di Mambro hit back at the Dutoit family by telling his followers that the Dutoit child was the Antichrist and would try to overthrow his daughter one day. Not long after, he flew two members of his inner circle from Switzerland to Quebec to assassinate the Dutoit family. Their bodies were found in Morin Heights on 4 October 1994. The two charred bodies that were found in the same chalet as the Dutoit family were Gerry Geroud and Colette Rochat. They were members of the cult but were not the killers, and the police never quite understood why they were in the house. One theory is that they may have set fire to the house before they committed suicide, in the hope that police would not realize that the Dutoit family had been targeted. As Quebecois police tried to piece together the tragedy that had taken place, they were shocked to learn that, thousands of miles away in Switzerland, a very serious incident had occurred which had strange similarities to their case.

It had taken place in the small town of Cheiry in Switzerland. A farmhouse belonging to local farmer Albert Giacobino was on fire and, as firemen searched the house for casualties, they came across his charred body. They were just about to declare the incident a suicide when they discovered that his house had been rigged with incendiary devices. Fearing the worst, they searched the outhouses on the property and came across a garage that, despite being empty, appeared to have hosted a number of people as there were various personal belongings strewn around the room.

Confused, but ever meticulous, an inspector noticed that something was not right about the garage and he soon realised that the outside of its structure was substantially larger than the room on the inside. Gathering a team together, they tested the density of the walls inside and before long they found that one was hollow. Upon inspection, they noticed that a portion of the suspicious wall was not fixed in place and they pulled it to the side. What they found was beyond anything they could have imagined. It was as if they had been transported into a medieval witchcraft film.

Behind the wall was a secret room. Its walls were lined with red drapes and mirrors and its floor, covered with a thick, blood red carpet. In the middle of the room there was a triangular altar, around which eighteen bodies were arranged on the floor. Like the spokes of a wheel, they formed a circle with their heads pointing outwards, covered in plastic bags. The bodies were clothed in long cloaks and ritual robes of lush red and gold material. Scattered around the room were champagne bottles and pools of blood that flowed from the headshot wounds that most of the victims had sustained. As if this discovery was not enough, four further bodies were found in a second room at the back and they later realised that the area surrounding the garage had also been rigged with explosives that had failed to go off.

As the days passed, the autopsies revealed that some of the victims had, indeed, been shot and others had either died of tranquiliser ingestion or suffocation. A few of the victims had bruising and some had been drugged prior to death, which baffled investigators even more. Were these deaths suicide, murder or both?

Although Swiss police had not linked these deaths with those in Quebec, they knew they had a major problem on their hands when, the next day, in the sleepy skiing town of Salvan, three adjacent ski chalets were set on fire. They made yet another gruesome discovery when they found twenty-five bodies inside, some of which were children. Cause of death was almost identical to victims found the day before; most had been shot in the head and drugged prior to death. It took very little time for Swiss authorities to link the incidents when it emerged that all the victims were members of a secretive cult, the Order of the Solar Temple. Autopsies soon revealed that the majority of those who died in the two incidents did not commit willing suicide. Most believed that they were attending a ceremony, and were murdered upon arrival by the fanatical killers, who went on to take their own lives. Some of the victims were successful members of society, including a mayor, a journalist and a civil servant. Police had initially believed that Jouret and Di Mambro had orchestrated the deaths and fled the country, but they were later identified as being among the dead in Switzerland. Did they believe in their own doctrines so fully that they were prepared to die? Or did they kill themselves knowing that their fate had been sealed?

Once the deaths in Quebec and Switzerland were had been linked to the cult, authorities on both sides of the Atlantic continued to work together to try and solve these crimes, which were now under the media's spotlight worldwide.

It would be just over a year later, on 15 December 1995, that the Solar Temple would make a statement once more when sixteen members were found dead in the forested town of Vercors, France. Most had been drugged prior to death and their bodies had been arranged in the same wheel formation as those in Cheiry. Three of the victims were children, one of whom was just eighteen months old. One of the adults who had supervised the murders and suicides turned out to be a police officer and suicide notes were found at several of the victims' homes, in which they stated their desire to travel to a new world.

On 22 March 1997, five bodies were found in an incinerated house in Saint-Casimir, Quebec. All had been drugged and four had arranged their bodies in the shape of a cross, while the fifth had a plastic bag over her head. They later learnt that these plastic bags symbolised an ecological disaster that they believed would destroy the human race. When they searched the perimeter, they found three teenagers in a workshop next door. They had been drugged but were still alive, having convinced their parents to let them escape.

As several countries worked together to put the cases to rest, they learned that Jouret and Di Mambro had organised a Last Supper with twelve of their followers prior to the night of their deaths in Switzerland. A recording was later found that revealed the message that they shared with their flock, to persuade them that death had become their only option.

> We are rejected by the whole world. First by the people, the people can no longer withstand us. And our Earth, fortunately she rejects us. How would we leave [otherwise]? We also reject this planet. We wait for the day we can leave... life for me is intolerable, intolerable, I can't go on. So think about the dynamic that will get us to go elsewhere.

But was there more to the story? Were these really just the actions of two crazed cult fanatics who led their gullible flock to their deaths? As the investigations came to a close, multiple factors were brought to light that revealed disturbing insight into the mindset of the cult leaders in the year before their deaths.

From Di Mambro's perspective, he felt as if he had reached the end of his rope. It was little known that he had been seriously ill in the years before his death. He was suffering with kidney failure and had been diagnosed with cancer. To add to his woes, both his children had begun to rebel against him, with his son wanting nothing more to do with his scams and his daughter becoming increasingly unwilling to continue her role as future messiah. For Jouret, things had gone downhill as well. His status as leader and prophet was crumbling due to recent stories being circulated by ex-members, including Tony Dutoit's accusation that the spirits he conjured were nothing but a big deception. He lost credibility after his arrest in Quebec and his once motivational speeches seemed to no longer have any effect on his flock.

Moreover, the two leaders were no longer in sync and had been in a psychological battle against each other for the last few years. With Di Mambro now in his seventies and with his health failing, Jouret believed he should relinquish control and leave him to run the cult. But the older man was not prepared to do so.

Negative press and investigations into their practises and finances had left them both feeling persecuted by a world that they believed was out to destroy them. They knew it was only a matter of time before the law caught up with them. After all, the two men had been extorting money from their followers for quite a few years and had been less than honest when declaring their assets for tax purposes.

They knew that in certain countries, police had tapped their 'phones and were monitoring their movements, which made them more paranoid than ever. A file was found on Di Mambro's computer which highlights his delusional state of mind in the months before the mass suicides and murders.

> We don't know when they might close the trap on us. A few days? A few weeks? We are being followed and spied upon in our every move. All the cars are equipped with tracing and listening devices. All of their most sophisticated techniques are being used on us. While in the house, beware of surveillance cameras, lasers, and infra-red. Our file is the hottest on the planet, the most important of the last ten years, if not of the century. However that may be, as it turns out, the concentration of hate against us will give us enough energy to leave.

Another demonstration of their paranoia was revealed in a letter that Di Mambro sent to a French minister, in which he attempted to blame him for their decision to die.

> We accuse you of having attempted to deliberately destroy our Order for reasons of state... we accuse you of premeditated group murder. As a result, we have decided to leave the terrestrial plane ahead of time because we are aware of your desire to destroy the Work we have accomplished.

To make matters worse, just a year earlier the Branch Davidians had committed their final act of defiance against the US government when seventy-six members of their cult died in a fire at their ranch, following a lengthy media-covered stand-off with local police. This incident prompted a wave of negativity towards cults in general, which caused the Solar Temple to lose a number of their disciples, resulting in a massive drop in their financial income. The future of their brotherhood was under threat and it was too late to steer their remaining flock into a new direction.

Appallingly, it appears that the perverse cult leaders were actually jealous of the tragedy at Waco. In a recorded conversation, they can be heard voicing their envy at the fact that Davidian cult leader, David Koresh, had in some way robbed them of their thunder.

> Di Mambro: People have beaten us to the punch, you know.
>
> Jouret: Well, yeah. Waco beat us to the punch.
>
> Di Mambro: In my opinion, we should have gone six months before them... what we'll do will be even more spectacular!

It seems that the jig was up. Both Di Mambro and Jouret knew that their time as wealthy and powerful cult leaders was over. Rather than fade into retirement, they decided to put an end to their lives and order the self-destruction of their cult in the process. Truly, Jouret lived up to his own quote:

> Liberation is not where human beings think it is. Death can represent an essential stage of life.

As for those who willingly took their lives or participated in the murders, I can only imagine that, throughout their years while under the cult's influence, they had reached a point of no return psychologically. Over time, the cult leadership had very much isolated their members from the outside world, as so often occurs in a cult environment. Through their teachings, they encouraged segregation and instilled in their followers a feeling of non-belonging to the world and its realities. They spread their paranoia to all their members, convincing them that governments around the world were spying on them and were out to destroy them. This only heightened their followers' sense of belonging to this special brotherhood and their feeling that they must be a part of something so powerful that it warranted the government's attention. So much so that, by the time the leaders announced they all had to leave their earthly bodies, most already felt as if they no longer belonged in them. Jouret and Di Mambro were so obsessed with leaving behind a legacy that they sent letters to the media, justifying their actions, as if somehow they felt that no one would understand their twisted reasoning behind the transits. They were right. Nothing the public discovered about their doctrines made their actions any less depraved and egoist.

In 1990, authorities arrested Michael Tabachnik, a famous Swiss musician and conductor, who was rumoured to be the new leader of the cult and to have been involved in the planning of the transits. But, with no concrete evidence of his involvement, he was cleared of all charges. The best the authorities could do was to try and provide the victims' families with some idea of what had taken place. However, with most key players dead, they had to speculate on some details. In some cases, it was quite clear who had willingly died and who had been murdered but in others it was difficult to tell.

When the investigators from Quebec, Switzerland and France shared their findings, it was established that they could clearly separate the dead into three distinct groups. The 'Awakened' were the first group, which contained those who were part of the inner circle of the cult and who had committed most of the murders, before ending their own lives. The second, the 'Immortals', were shot or suffocated to death. It is speculated that they were given the option of suicide but several were murdered when they appeared to lack the nerve to go through with it. The third group comprised the 'Traitors', a small portion of the dead who, unlike the Immortals, had been assassinated in cold blood, most likely as the leaders felt that they had somehow betrayed the cult.

The Order of the Solar Temple left behind a terrible legacy with a total death count of seventy-four people who had been murdered or who had committed suicide between 1994 and 1997. As far as we know, the movement has since disbanded and its members have reintegrated into society. Occasionally, however, a rumour will surface, claiming that they are still active to this day. One can only hope that, if they are, they will never make headline news again.

CHAPTER 13

Heaven's Gate:
Marshall Applewhite

As I researched the inner workings and ultimate demise of the bizarre cult, Heaven's Gate, I could not help but note some similarities with the Order of the Solar Temple. Not only did they exist and commit their fatal acts around the same time but some of the characteristics of their belief system bear an uncanny resemblance.

Texan Marshall Applewhite was born 17 May 1931. He was the son of a Presbyterian minister who engrained religion into him from a young age. In what appeared to be a promising start in life, Applewhite excelled in his studies and earned himself a bachelor's degree in philosophy in 1952. At first, he planned to become a minister, but then he changed his mind and decided instead that he wanted to start a career in music. He married Anne Pearce in his early twenties and they went on to have two children together.

After studying at the University of Colorado, he earned a master's degree in music and went on to start a respectable career working as a music teacher at the University of Alabama. But his seemingly perfect life crumbled a few years later, when he was fired from his job for having an affair with a male student. When his wife learnt of his infidelity she left him and began divorce proceedings. Applewhite moved to Houston, where he found another position as a music teacher and spent most of his spare time volunteering as the choral director of his local church. During this time, he had relationships with both men and women, all of which were unsuccessful. It is at this stage that people around him began to notice that he appeared confused and, at times, incoherent, as if he were lost in another world. There are rumours that he engaged in a sexual relationship with one of his female students, which forced him to leave his job again. He spent a few months in New Mexico before returning to Texas around the time that his father died.

Broke and jobless, his father's death hit him hard. His psychological state seems to have changed dramatically from this point and he admitted himself into a psychiatric hospital to seek help for depression and his obsession with sex. He began to reject traditional Christian concepts that he had been taught as a child and, instead, he looked for answers in the paranormal and astrology. Had he been left to his own devices, he no doubt would have continued his mental descent until he would have eventually been admitted into an institution for treatment. That is, had he not met Bonnie Nettles. It was a chance encounter that would change the course of his life and set into motion a sequence of events that would end tragically.

In 1972, Applewhite suffered a heart attack and was admitted to hospital for recovery. There he met nurse Nettles, who listened intently as he told her about a near-death experience that he claimed to have had. He described a vision that he had seen, in which it was revealed to him that they were the 'two witnesses', the prophets that would herald the end of the world according to the biblical Book of Revelation. Before meeting Applewhite, Nettles had already taken a keen interest in the occult and considered herself an intensely spiritual person. This meant she bonded with her patient almost instantly. She told him that she had been forewarned of their meeting by extra terrestrials who had spoken of a great mission that they would carry out together.

Their relationship grew from there and Applewhite moved into her residence shortly after. Nettles' husband left her, taking their children with him, which left her free to embark on a wild journey of mystic discovery with her new friend. Their relationship was not physical, but one of two minds who believed beyond doubt that they were soul mates and deeply connected on a spiritual level. By early 1973, they were no longer content to keep their doctrines to themselves and they launched out on a road trip across several states, where they tried to spread their beliefs and win over converts. It was a difficult journey. With hardly any money, they wandered around with no real organisation or plan to fall back on. They slept where they could—in campsites, cheap motels or, at times, out in the open and they worked odd jobs to earn enough money to eat.

Their insistence paid off when, the following year, they managed to win over one of their friends who became their first disciple. By this point, their doctrines had somewhat diverted from biblical teachings, particularly as they had become rather obsessed with science fiction and jointly believed that their role as the two witnesses meant that they had been blessed with supernatural intelligence.

This led Applewhite to become convinced that he was the direct descendant of Jesus Christ and that he and Nettles would eventually die as martyrs and be resurrected before being transported on to an alien spaceship. They made an attempt to preach their message to other religious groups but, unsurprisingly, they were not well received and negative press was written about them. It is very likely that Applewhite was suffering from increasingly regular delusions and hallucinations which with Nettles' encouragement, had become part of his reality.

Applewhite was arrested and jailed for six months in 1974 after he failed to return a rental car. After being detained, he told police that he had received divine authorisation to keep the car, which obviously failed to get him off the hook. While incarcerated, he used his time to research further concepts to enhance the doctrines of his cult. His belief in aliens grew immensely and, by the time he was released, he claimed that he and Nettles had undergone a transformation. They had become 'walk-ins', a trending concept amongst sci-fi fans and New Age spiritual groups. It meant that their souls had been removed from their bodies and an extra-terrestrial being had taken its place, occupying their every thought and action. It was an extreme way of distancing themselves from their past teachings up until that date. After all, anything they had previously predicted that had not come true could now be dismissed as being the work of the human occupiers that preceded them. They were also free to change their future teachings under the pretext that they were now inhabited by superior alien minds.

With this transformation came the revelation that they had been chosen to select a team of spiritually advanced souls to take with them when they returned to their UFO. According to their new belief, their alien ancestors had created the world long ago but had now returned to destroy it, as it had become too polluted and filled with spiritual sin. After the apocalyptic destruction of earth had taken place, they would rejuvenate it and then return to their own alien planet. Those who followed their teachings would be a part of that elite team who would be saved from the doom that was about to befall the earth. Their mission was to spend their every moment preparing their minds and souls for their journey into the next world.

On their website, there is a page entitled 'Statement by an E.T. presently incarnate', which is both amusing and incredulous, but also riddled with conspiracy theories to explain how the co-leaders arrived on earth and what their mission was. Reading it, I felt as if I had stepped into an episode of the *X-Files* series, but with a truckload of religion mixed in. However, it must have captured the interest of some minds as they recruited several followers with whom they lived communally. Unlike most cults, both leaders appeared to have no interest in financial wealth and they lived frugally amongst their disciples, often getting by on the bare minimum.

Applewhite taught his followers that the human body was a vehicle, a vessel that carried their souls. In order to earn their place as a survivor before the destruction of earth, they had to achieve what he called the 'Next Level'. Members had to reject all physical ties including sex, material possessions, wealth, family, friends and careers. Only then would they be prepared to be transported to the UFO, where the aliens would transform them into their extra-terrestrial bodies.

As for their previous prediction that they would be martyred, Applewhite had an answer as to why that had not occurred. He told his followers that it had actually happened, but not in the way that they thought it would. He went on to explain that the bad press the group had previously received was a form of martyrdom and, hence, his prophecy had come true after all. It was a lousy cover-up, but it seemed to do the trick.

By 1975, they had around 100 members in their group. Many were young students who had been won over by Applewhite's 'no pressure' approach, while others rushed to join when the cult leaders publically announced the landing of a UFO in September of that year. They named their group the Anonymous Sexaholics Celibate Church before renaming it Human Individual Metamorphosis. The co-leaders also gave themselves the nicknames Bo and Peep which they later changed to Do and Ti, and encouraged their followers to adopt new names that ended in '-ody'.

The spaceship didn't land that September and a steady stream of followers left the cult, leaving Applewhite with around two dozen members. Living like gypsies, they wandered around campsites for the next three years, increasingly withdrawn from the eyes of the world Although Applewhite was said to be a very relaxed person who adopted a familiar and close relationship with his followers, he could also be rather removed from their daily lives and regularly communicated with them through his personal assistant, or through Nettles. He often portrayed a lack of consistency in his behaviour when it came to the rules that he imposed upon his disciples. One example of this was the strict control he had over members' day-to-day activities, despite his insistence that no one was forced to follow his rules. He would rarely tell any of them what to do, but instead would offer them a choice, knowing full well that they would obey him anyway. It was quite a clever method of mind control. By brainwashing them with his doctrines, and yet allowing them what appeared to be freedom, their loyalty for him only grew stronger.

The two leaders often tested their flock to see just how far they were willing to go for them. One afternoon, they gathered their followers and told them that a UFO would be landing that night and that they should wait outside for it. The next morning, no one had budged from their position. They were standing together in the same spot, cold and hungry, when Applewhite finally called them inside and, with great pride, congratulated them on passing the test. He knew that he had them just where he wanted them. They were so focused on their mission that they would do anything to achieve it.

By the mid-1980s, the cult community was tight-knit and operating smoothly. Applewhite had allowed members to keep their outside jobs in order to provide for the commune financially but, apart from that, they had little contact with the outside world, including their own relatives. However, in 1983, he allowed them to return to their families for Mother's Day. He put strict limitations on the period of time they were allowed to stay away and told them to tell their family members that they were at a computer school. These trips were both to reassure their families that they were fine and to give cult members the illusion that they were being allowed freedom.

Later that year, Nettles had to have an eye surgically removed due to a cancer that she had been fighting for several years. The operation was a success, but the cancer was aggressive and she eventually succumbed to the disease in 1985. When she passed away, she left a devastated Applewhite behind. Despite his followers' best attempts to comfort him, the cult leader became very depressed. However, he maintained his leadership, using Nettles' death as another opportunity to convince them of their mission. He told them that Nettles had become so powerful spiritually that her body could no longer handle it and, therefore, she was sent to the Next Level. He began to refer to her as 'the Father' as he was convinced that she was now spiritually superior to him. However, deep down inside he was worried that her death may trigger the collapse of the cult. He became more controlling and decided to arrange marriages between his followers in a mock ceremony, hoping that it would increase their unity.

To maintain his own position, he elevated himself to the level of Christ, claiming that salvation could only come through him as he was now the sole mediator between them and their extra-terrestrial creators. He demanded more loyalty and submission from his disciples, which transformed the dynamics of the group. After Nettles' death, he became increasingly paranoid. He spoke to his followers of evil aliens called Luciferians, who he believed were trying to infiltrate the cult under human disguise. He shut the doors of their commune, refusing to allow any outsiders within their property and was hesitant to accept new members into his group. He compared his cult to the Jewish zealots at Masada who held off the Romans' invasion until their deaths by group suicide. He also spoke more regularly of the apocalypse, increasingly certain that it was now about to befall them.

He went on to amend his theory on how they would be transported to the Next Level. Previously, he had told them that their alien creators would descend on earth to take them in their human form and that only when they had been transported to their spaceship, would they be changed into extra-terrestrials.

But, in light of Nettles' death, he spoke of it from a more spiritual angle, telling his disciples that their human bodies would be left behind as their spirits alone would be lifted to the spaceship, where it would be placed inside their new body. They would then travel to heaven, which, according to Applewhite, was another planet in the universe that was occupied by Next Level beings, just like the ones that they would be transformed into.

He compared the transformation to the death of Jesus Christ, whom he believed was an extra-terrestrial that was sent to earth to take humans back to their planet of origin. But, in his opinion, this could not take place in AD 33, as Jesus found that the human race was not spiritually prepared enough to be transformed. In his version of events, Christ rose from the dead in the form of an alien and was carried away on a spaceship. Now, nearly 2,000 years later, he believed that humans were being given another chance to reach that infamous Next Level, but that only he and his followers were perceptive enough to see this opportunity. Because of this, they were able to prepare their minds and souls under Applewhite's leadership and earn themselves their salvation from the destruction and remodelling of the earth.

By the late 1980s, the cult had become a group of recluses. So much so, that most people had forgotten that they even existed. That is until 1992 when, having lost the majority of his flock, Applewhite decided to launch a recruitment campaign. They broadcasted a video series by satellite explaining their doctrines and spent $30,000 on an advert in *USA Today* magazine, which warned of the end of the world. Around twenty ex-members returned to the cult following the campaign and a small cluster of new disciples also joined, which brought their numbers back up to around fifty. They went on to hold public lectures under their new name, Total Overcomers Anonymous, and posted their teachings on the internet. However, they received a lot of criticism in response, which discouraged Applewhite greatly. He began to realise that the general public would never accept his doctrines and teachings and that they would always think of him as a UFO-obsessed cult leader.

Not long after this, he began to speak of suicide as a possible way of attaining the Next Level and he changed the name of their cult to Heaven's Gate. With time passing and no sign of the aliens, he warned his followers that they may have to be prepared to give up their human bodies in order to make the transition.

In June 1995, the cult attempted to build a compound out of tyres and lumber in a forty-acre plot that they had bought in New Mexico. But the project had to be abandoned when Applewhite's health deteriorated and, instead, they decided to move to a rented mansion in Rancho Santa Fe, California. There, Applewhite made the decision to undergo voluntary castration as he believed that aliens had no gender. The fact that he made this decision is quite surprising as many cult leaders do not live by their own doctrines, let alone voluntarily carry out such an extreme procedure in order to prove their belief in their own teachings. In my opinion, this suggests that Applewhite was suffering from severe mental illness by this stage. Many cult leaders believe in their own doctrines to some extent, but are essentially con artists who gain from their position as leaders. Applewhite was, at that point, so deluded that he was entirely convinced in his own theories and lived them as fully as he expected his followers to. It was as if he had managed to brainwash himself. It appears that his followers were just as influenced by him. They began to look alike, wearing similar clothing and hairstyles. Seven of his male disciples even went so far as to undergo voluntary castration after he had been through the procedure.

By November 1996, Applewhite had something entirely new to focus on when it was announced that the comet Hale-Bopp would be passing near the earth, an event that he believed was of great significance. The last time that this comet had travelled near our planet was in 2,200 BC and astrologers at the time believed that it heralded the arrival of a man who would bring peace in the world and deliver the truth to all nations. This time, Applewhite and other New Age groups believed that its passing signalled the beginning of the final three and a half years of Satan's reign on earth. Convinced that his theory was right, his group announced the joyous news on their website and they spent $10,000 taking out alien abduction insurance for all their members.

Their elation only increased when mathematician and scientist, Dr Courtney Brown, went public with photographs of the moving comet that appeared to show an object following it. The scientist believed that it may be a UFO and the Heaven's Gate community could not have been more relieved. After years of preparation, their spaceship was finally *en route* and they celebrated by watching their favourite movie, *Star Wars,* and spending the day at a UFO conference.

A few days later, however, when the infamous photo was analysed, it was quickly assessed as a hoax. Applewhite and his followers did not let that cool their enthusiasm and, instead, they insisted that their spaceship was well and truly on its way to them, whether it was visible or not. On the homepage of their website they wrote:

Whether Hale-Bopp has a 'companion' or not is irrelevant from our perspective. However, its arrival is joyously very significant to us at Heaven's Gate. The joy is that our Older Member in the Evolutionary Level Above Human (the 'Kingdom of Heaven') has made it clear to us that Hale-Bopp's approach is the 'marker' we've been waiting for—the time for the arrival of the spacecraft from the Level Above Human to take us home to 'Their World'—in the literal Heavens. Our 22 years of classroom here on planet Earth is finally coming to conclusion—'graduation' from the Human Evolutionary Level. We are happily prepared to leave 'this world' and go with Ti's crew.

If you study the material on this website you will hopefully understand our joy and what our purpose here on Earth has been. You may even find your 'boarding pass' to leave with us during this brief window. We are so very thankful that we have been recipients of this opportunity to prepare for membership in Their Kingdom, and to experience Their boundless Caring and Nurturing.

Hale-Bopp was scheduled to be at its closest distance to earth on 22 March 1997 and the group of believers were not about to miss their flight. The evening before, they finalised their plans and Applewhite sat down with thirty-eight of his most ardent followers for their last supper. They ate chicken pies, salads and cheesecakes. The next day, they woke and calmly dressed in identical outfits—black shirts, black sweat pants and brand new black and white trainers. On their left sleeve was stitched, 'Heaven's Gate Away Team' and they placed a five dollar bill and three quarters in their shirt pocket, as was standard practice whenever a cult member left the compound. They packed a small bag with clothing, lip balm and a notebook, which they placed at the end of their beds, leaving a form of identification somewhere nearby where it could be easily found.

Four days later, police broke into the mansion after receiving alarming information from two ex-cult members which suggested that the Heaven's Gate cult had committed mass suicide. Applewhite had sent them both a videotaped recording, which revealed their plans. Even before they entered the house, the stench of decomposing bodies was apparent. When they moved through the rooms they were horrified to find that the residents of the house were all dead, their bodies had been neatly arranged on their beds with purple shrouds placed over them. They were perplexed by the identical outfits and, at first they mistakenly thought that all the victims were male as they all had identical short haircuts. However, they later realised this was not the case, as twenty-one of the thirty-nine Caucasian bodies found were female.

Initially, police were certain that this was yet another group suicide orchestrated by the Order of the Solar Temple, whose members had been carrying out multiple suicides over the past three years. The bizarre ritualistic set-up of the bodies appeared alike and there were similarities in the reasons that were given on Applewhite's video recording, as both cults spoke of transformations that would have to take place in order to travel to another planet. But the investigation soon revealed their true identity and incredibly farfetched beliefs. On that fateful day, fifteen cult members were chosen to be a part of the first team that would be transported to the spaceship. They were given a lethal dose of an anticonvulsant drug, barbiturate phenobarbital, which had been mixed with fruit puree and which they washed down with vodka. All fifteen then covered their heads with plastic bags to enable themselves to pass out more quickly.

Once they were unconscious, those still alive removed the bags and covered each one with a purple shroud, leaving them to die of the toxic substance.

The following day, another team of fifteen repeated the same process and, the day after that, a final team of nine cult members followed suit. The investigation concluded that all of his followers died willingly, and even appeared eager and excited about their deaths in videotape recordings that were later found.

In his final recorded speech entitled 'Do's Final Exit', it is sadly evident that Applewhite is not in full possession of his mental faculties. With a crazed expression, he stares into the camera lens, his eyes wild and devoid of any connection to reality.

> Part of our test of faith is our hating this world, even our flesh body, enough to be willing to leave it without any proof other than what we have come to know.

It is obvious that he is fully convinced of his own message and that he has lost all sense and reason. After so many years of living in a world of aliens and conspiracy theories, his already fragile psyche was pushed into complete delusion.

As details emerged over the next few months, the authorities and the public realised that this seemingly harmless and secluded group of alien fanatics were really not as innocent as they had appeared to be. The mass suicide had been carefully planned for many years before it took place and the cult leaders had brainwashed their disciples into believing their incredulous theories. So much so that, just a few weeks later, two former members of the cult attempted to commit suicide by following a similar process in a hotel room in Encinitas. One was successful. His wife had passed away in the initial batch of suicides and he was determined to join her. The second man didn't die, but the following year he pumped exhaust fumes into his car in the middle of the Arizona desert and finally achieved his goal. A purple shroud was found next to him in the car.

After the media storm subsided, Heaven's Gate was never heard of again. Their website is still active and the domain has been maintained, which may be down to former members who are still sympathetic towards their cause. Many believe that what was left of the group died on that day, with no survivors left to keep the cult going. Others claim that they are still active, but have changed their name and live in secrecy.

In 2012, some 200 hippies camped out at the base of Pic de Bugarach mountain in the south of France. They claimed that their extra-terrestrial founders had hidden a spaceship in the mountain, which would emerge on 21 December of that year to take them back to their alien planet. It is not known whether they were members of Heaven's Gate, but I can confirm that there was no spaceship or supernatural pick-up that day.

In my opinion, the main difference between Applewhite and many other cult leaders is that he was known to be mentally ill and had even sought psychiatric help for himself on several occasions. I believe that he was entirely convinced that his mission was real and that he was going to be transported to a spaceship after his death. I do wonder if perhaps the individual we should look more closely at is his colleague, Nettles. Although she was clearly obsessed with the supernatural and aliens, she was not insane. But she did encourage Applewhite to act upon his delusions and persuaded him to create a cult and then drag innocent people into a world of fantasy that ended in tragedy. Was she the driving force behind the movement? Did her death drive Applewhite to seek the only way out that he knew? We will never know.

CHAPTER 14

Movement for the Restoration of the Ten Commandments of God
Joseph Kibweteere and Credonia Mwerinde

On a warm day in March 2000, local authorities in Kanunga, Uganda, made a horrifying discovery. Alerted by the sound of an explosion and the putrid smell of burning flesh, they advanced slowly into a cult-owned compound and began to scan though the buildings on the property. When they reached the church, they found mounds of charred skulls and incinerated bodies, many of which belonged to children. Located amongst beautiful rolling hills and plantations, the cult property would reveal itself to be a mass graveyard, as the secrets buried beneath its red dirt were brought to the surface.

Some years prior, in 1989, Joseph Kibweteere, a wealthy former Catholic Priest who had been expelled from the Church, met thirty-seven-year-old former prostitute turned religious fanatic, Credonia Mwerinde, who claimed to be in direct contact with the Virgin Mary. Mwerinde had been immersed in religion from a young age by her father, Paul Kashaku, who claimed to be a seer who had also experienced visions of the Virgin Mary.

She had married five times before she turned her life around after a series of spiritual experiences. Her father encouraged her to spread her testimony around Uganda and it was during her travels that she met the man who would be the co-founder of their cult. With her father's encouragement, they formed the Movement for the Restoration of the Ten Commandments of God and, before long, they attracted numerous followers, many of whom were either disillusioned or had been excommunicated from the Catholic Church.

Uganda had been through a dark period and its people were desperate for anything that would bring them hope. Idi Amin's reign of terror had left the country in disarray and turmoil. Crime, poverty and disease were still rife across the country and many had lost confidence in their government. Mwerinde and Kibweteere offered salvation and a communal lifestyle in which their followers shared everything and worked together for common goals. This concept was very attractive to many, particularly to those who still lived in fear that another oppressive tyrant may take control of the country and rule with brutality, as Amin had done. The cult's community was a shelter where they could feel safe and protected from the evil that they had so often seen around them.

As their following grew, they nominated three of their disciples to help them manage the leadership of the group. Joseph Kasapurari, John Kamagara and Dominic Kataribabo, all former Catholic Priests, became joint leaders, though the two original founders very much remained at the top of the hierarchy. With increasing numbers of new disciples came an influx of finances. Everyone who joined their church had to immediately sell everything including their land, personal belongings and vehicles; the profit from these sales and any other savings they had went into the community's common pot. Before long, they had raised enough money to buy a large property surrounded by plantations in Rwashamaire, which they turned into their residence. They also opened several offices in Western Uganda, which were used for fundraising and recruitment.

Their doctrines were very similar to those of the Catholic Church, apart from the immense focus they placed on following the Ten Commandments. They believed that the only way to avoid damnation was to strictly follow those ten rules and they took this belief to the extreme, banning their followers from engaging in sexual intercourse and even forbidding them to talk, out of fear that they may break the ninth commandment, 'Thou shalt not bear false witness against thy neighbour'. During these long periods of silence, members were to communicate using sign language. They were also forbidden to use soap and had to wear uniforms—green for general members and black for the leaders. They were given two meals a day, except for Fridays and Mondays, on which they were only given one. Families were often split up and sent to separate cult camps, particularly if one of the parents began to have doubts. Children were disciplined by the leaders and senior members of the church, who had authority over just about anyone they deemed in need of correction.

Around this time, Mwerinde claimed that she was receiving messages from the Virgin Mary via the electronic equipment in her home, such as the radio or television. She and her co-leaders began to preach of the end of the world, which they said would take place on 31 December 1999, on the eve of the new millennium. They told their followers that, like Noah in the Bible, they too would be the only righteous ones to be saved and would be the sole survivors left to repopulate the world. They issued a booklet entitled, 'A Timely Message from Heaven: The End of the Present Time,' which they required all newcomers to read over and over again before their membership could be confirmed. At this point, it is estimated that they had up to 5,000 members of various levels. Some continued their regular lifestyle and simply attended their sermons, but other more dedicated members lived in the cult's compound and devoted their entire lives to the group.

In excerpts of their booklet, we can clearly see the leadership's attempt to spread panic and fear amongst their flock in a bid to draw them into their fold.

> The Lord told me that hurricanes of fire would rain forth from heaven and spread over all those who would not have repented. They would burn them but would not die immediately... This fire will also reach inside the buildings; there is no way one can escape. Those who had repented were told to go in hiding to the houses they had built for this purpose. These houses are called 'Ark' or 'Ship'.
>
> We are definitely taking you to Jesus through the Blessed Virgin Mary, who have commissioned us, and through the Pope. Since the Ten Commandments of God have been abandoned and are being broken, those who go to hell are very many... Those going to heaven are few. Ours is not a religion but a movement that endeavours to make the people aware of the fact that the Commandments of God have been abandoned, and it gives what should be done for their observance.
>
> A great number of youths now move about more or less naked. They move about putting on slit-skirts, see-through dresses without any under-clothing. Some move about half-naked putting on back-show dresses. Girls prefer wearing men's trousers to wearing their own dresses... All these are symptoms of an urge to violate the Sixth Commandment. Our Blessed Mother Mary says that we, the youths, are like simpletons or fools because of having allowed Satan to dwell in us and make us do all sorts of shameful actions.
>
> AIDS ... is a disaster that has befallen the world. AIDS is a punishment that has been released to the world due to its disobedience. The sole cure is repenting our disobedience, and the restoration of the Ten Commandments of God.

However, in 1992, they were forced to abandon their large property in Rwashamaire as local villagers grew suspicious of their activities and made it difficult for them to operate. They sold the property and moved over 300 cult members to an even larger compound in Kanungu district. There, surrounded by beautiful hills, they built an entire village complete with residential houses, a school and a church. They were quite organised and aimed to be as self-sufficient as possible. Most cult members were assigned to agricultural work in the fields and plantations on the compound, while others specialised in childcare, administration, construction or farming cattle. Their working hours were gruelling and they were rarely allowed a day off. Even the children were put to work, regardless of their age.

They built a high, double fence around the property to ensure the privacy of its residents and to allow them to carry out their religious practices in secret.

The leaders began to exert even more control over their followers. Mwerinde, now elevated as High Priestess of the movement, very much ran the church and steered it in whatever direction she chose by claiming that holy messages from the Virgin Mary were guiding her. Kibweteere, however, was more of a puppet leader; he enjoyed exerting control over their followers, but did not have much say in the decisions that were made about the running of the cult or its spiritual direction. As a man, he commanded more respect, particularly due to his previous career as a priest, which made his presence as co-leader essential, if only for appearances. Reports later indicated that, despite banning all members from engaging in sexual intercourse, Mwerinde and Kibweteere were in fact lovers. They were caught in bed on several occasions but witnesses were ordered to keep quiet, with threat of punishment if they spoke of what they had seen.

Overall, the cult kept to itself and the majority of its members had little to no contact with the outside world. They were made to cut ties with their relatives, even if they lived in the town just outside the compound. Although the villagers in the surrounding areas thought they were odd, they gave them the benefit of the doubt and paid little attention to their activities.

In 1998, the commune's school was shut down when an inspection found the conditions of the building to be unsanitary. They had also heard rumours of child abuse, which they investigated. The cult leaders responded in an extremely friendly and open way, demonstrating great readiness to accept advice and to follow their recommendations of changes that needed to be made. They refuted all claims of child maltreatment and allowed inspectors to question smiling parents and children to dissipate the allegations. Their ploy worked and they were allowed to reopen the school shortly after. It would later emerge that authorities had only seen a small selection of the more healthy-looking children. Witnesses claimed to have seen severely malnourished children who were in poor health and hardly ever spoke, out of fear of being beaten. It is likely that the authorities were lenient with the cult due to its reputation among local police and government officials. In a bid to avoid suspicion, cult followers regularly participated in community work and Kibweteere discreetly paid out bribes to influential politicians in their district.

Two years later, as the apocalyptic deadline approached, the cult suddenly ceased all agricultural work and began to sell just about everything they owned. They flogged cattle and furniture at ridiculously cheap prices, at times asking for just a third of what it was worth. Some locals found this suspicious, but they didn't follow up on their concerns as they had been led to believe that the cult leaders were intending to buy several trucks for the commune. Within the compound, followers were made to confess their sins in an urgent bid to cleanse their souls and redeem themselves in the eyes of God. They spent long hours in fervent prayer and attended church sessions daily as the countdown continued.

As night fell on 31 December 1999, the community held their breaths and waited for the apocalypse to take place. As the hours passed, disappointment grew and, by dawn, they realised that the prophecy had failed to come true. Kibweteere and Mwerinde were immediately worried that they may have lost credibility and, in a bid to retain the devotion of their disciples, they told them that they had simply misunderstood the date that the Virgin Mary had given them. They assured them that the end of the world was indeed imminent, but that it would take place on 17 March 2000.

Understandably, some of their followers began to voice doubts about their leadership and the communications they claimed to be receiving from the Virgin Mary. Financial donations decreased significantly, as several of their sponsors dropped out and ex-members demanded the return of the assets that they had donated to the cult. But incredibly, the majority of their followers still believed. Perhaps they felt that they had no other option but to go along with it, given that they were completely tied to the group and did not have the financial means to escape.

Two days before the new predicted date, the leaders organised a big party. They roasted several bulls and spoilt their followers with mounds of food and soft drinks. After years of scarcely eating and living in poverty, this must have been quite the treat for unsuspecting cult members. They assumed that this celebration was merely in light of the joyous events to come; they could not have known what their leaders had planned for them.

On the morning of 17 March 2000, around 340 people entered church, of which 78 were children. Once inside, the windows and doors of the long wooden structure were boarded up as the large congregation burst into song and praise. Half an hour later, an explosion was heard by neighbours in surrounding properties. They noticed thick, black smoke rising from the compound and police were notified; however, by the time they reached the remote town, the blaze had subsided.

What they found inside was like nothing they had ever seen before. It was hard to even make out the bodies in the smouldering pile of ashes and bones. The fire had been so intense there was hardly anything left of those who had been inside. The explosion had caused the iron slabs of the church roof to cave in and the windows and door had been burnt to ashes.

It took several days to amass a team that was large enough to carry out a thorough search of the compound. When they did, they discovered eight more bodies that had been dumped in a cesspool beneath a toilet. In an attempt to hide the bodies, concrete had been clumsily spread over the hole. The police would soon realise that these bodies were the first of many more that they would find.

A week later, another mass grave was found in a cult commune located in Buhunga. Some 153 bodies had been buried in neat lines, most stacked in layers on top of each other. Fifty-nine of the victims were children and the remaining ninety-four were predominantly women.

A few days later, on 27 March, yet another mass grave was discovered, this time on cult leader Kataribabo's property in Rugazi. One hundred and fifty-five bodies were found buried in his yard and beneath his house. Another eighty-one bodies were discovered on the farm of a longstanding cult member in Rushojwa and, a few weeks after that, an additional fifty-five bodies were found at a cult residence in Buziga. The victims were of various ages and children were often found buried next to their parents.

With little resources and so many bodies to exhume, police called on prisons nearby to provide them with labourers to dig up the bodies. Barefooted and with no protective clothing, murderers, rapists and thieves dug through layers of dirt on the cult's properties, damaging much of the evidence in their effort. It caused quite a scandal when news agencies broadcast footage of this worldwide. However, the authorities did not have the manpower to exhume so many bodies and they had no choice but to continue as they were.

There was little evidence to go on and hardly any witnesses. The one thing that they were sure of was that, apart from those who died in the fire, most of the victims had been poisoned, stabbed, beaten or strangled to death. They also confirmed, by the degrees of decomposition, that the victims had been killed and buried in the year leading up to the fire. Some were in advanced stages of decomposition, whereas others had been buried only weeks prior. This finding led to even more questions. They had initially believed that they were dealing with a suicide, but now they were certain that the majority of the victims had not died willingly. To add to that, these murders had taken place over a period of months and the victims had been buried in an organised fashion. This was not a one-off killing spree, but mass murder that had been premeditated and carried out meticulously.

Neighbours who lived near cult properties were of little help. With high fences and shrubbery, most were unable to hear or see anything that had taken place within the compounds. But when investigating the church fire, authorities learnt that, just days earlier, Kataribabo had purchased fifty litres of sulphuric acid, which was possibly used to intensify the holocaust.

Although at first they were unsure if the church incident had been murder or suicide, they eventually concluded that the victims of the fire had not gone willingly to their deaths. It would seem that those who had entered the church that day were not aware of their leaders' intentions and went along in good faith, expecting a service followed by an apocalyptic event. Instead, they were boarded up inside and suffered a horrific death as they were burnt alive. Police also discovered mounds of charred toxic herbs nearby, which suggested that the victims may have been drugged by their fumes prior to entering the church.

One disciple, Ponsiano Nuwamanya, reported that, on the day of the fire, the cult leaders had sprinkled holy water on their breakfast. He did not find this unusual, but recalled that the water had a strange smell. He also told them that jerry cans of holy water had been placed in all four corners of the church before the prayer meeting, which he thought was odd as they had never done so before. But he had put it down to the imminent end of the world, an event which most likely required more holy water than usual.

He had an incredibly lucky escape. As some of the children in the church were crying, he had left the compound to buy them cakes in the nearby village. As he was leaving, he noticed that some of the men were boarding up the windows. He thought that it was simply part of their preparations for the Virgin Mary's arrival; assuming that the leaders wanted to leave their church safely locked behind them after they were taken to heaven.

He rushed back from the store, hoping that he had not missed the great event but, when he returned, the church was ablaze. He ran, fearing for his life, and sat in a field for hours in a state of shock before he regained his senses and sought out help. Nuwamanya also insisted that he had never heard talk of suicide during his time in the cult and he was certain that none of the other members were aware of their leaders' plans to end their lives.

It is very possible that the jerry cans were, in fact, filled with sulphuric acid and that the holy water sprinkled on the cult members' breakfasts was some type of sedative or poison. This could also explain in part why Nuwamanya found himself in a daze for hours following his escape; it could be that he was recovering from the effects of a toxin.

To this day, it is impossible to know exactly what went on inside the property in the months leading up to the fire as, to the best of our knowledge, all but one of the full-time members of the church were killed, either in the fire or in the year before. But the few details we do know demonstrate an environment in which no human rights were respected, down to the basic rights of individuals to speak, eat or engage in sexual activity with their partner. These small details indicate that it was an extremely oppressive and abusive situation, in which the leaders had full power and control over the spiritual and physical lives of their members. They treated them like slaves and had no regard for their wellbeing or happiness.

The final death count was around 800, although the actual number could be higher. Forensic experts claimed that some of the bodies were so effectively incinerated that their remains disintegrated entirely. In addition, there could be other mass graves that were never discovered. As for the depraved leaders who ran the cult, they are assumed to have perished in the fire, though there is no conclusive evidence of this as most bodies were so severely burnt that they could not be identified. Some claim it would have been impossible for them to escape without being seen, but many others are convinced that they went into hiding after carrying out the mass murders.

Kibweteere and Mwerinde, in particular, are still believed to be alive. When Nuwamanya was asked if they had died in the fire, he replied that they could not have, as he had seen several leaders leaving the compound earlier that morning. He said that Mwerinde had left instructions with two of her assistants before leaving the property, with the excuse that she needed to prepare another cult residence for the apocalypse. He also insisted that Kibweteere was not on the compound at all that day. International warrants of arrest were issued shortly after, but none of the leaders were ever found and the criminal case, although still officially open, appears to have gone cold.

So, what motivated these seemingly devout Christians to commit such heinous acts of murder? Some say that they were driven by wealth but, when we read about the impoverished conditions in which they lived, it is hard to believe that money would have been their primary motive. Even considering that their followers gave all their assets to the cult, their bank accounts would not have been that flush. After all, most of their disciples were poor villagers and farmers who would not have had much to contribute in the first place.

What does seem more likely is that the leaders simply reached that critical point that so many other destructive cult leaders eventually reach. They had promised their flock a haven, a place of spiritual wealth and communal bliss, where they would be taken care of and where their children would receive a good education. This alone would have lured a great number of impoverished believers into their church. But they were unable to deliver. Instead, they barely scraped by on donations and were continuously hit by suspicion from the outside world. That, coupled with their failed prediction would have made them feel as if their backs were up against the wall. If their second prediction was also proved wrong, the group would have disintegrated, resulting in demands for refunds and possibly criminal charges for child neglect, forced labour and embezzlement.

They were already on borrowed time and I believe that they decided to take the easy way out before they were exposed as frauds. Mwerinde had told her followers that, if her second prediction was proved wrong, they should stone her to death; I would hardly think that she would have allowed herself to meet that fate. Just before the tragedy, Kibweteere sent a letter to his estranged wife, who was no longer a member of the cult. In his letter, he begged her to continue what he had started, which is evidence that he was fully aware of the plans that had been put in place.

Those killed in the year prior to the fire were most likely disciples who had voiced doubts or expressed a desire to leave the cult. With the future of the movement looking very bleak, the twisted leaders would have found it easier to eliminate those who resisted them, rather than take the time to convince them to stay.

Some claim that Kibweteere suffered from bipolar disorder and, others, that he was a manic depressive. But his relatives insist that he was simply manipulated by Mwerinde, who apparently had complete control over him. It is hard to know, as there are so many inconsistencies in the information that has been discovered since the incident. It was later suggested that Mwerinde invented her past career as a prostitute in a bid to resemble Mary Magdalene. This ties in quite well with the rumour that she ran the cult almost exclusively and manipulated the other leaders into following her. Ex-cult members told investigators that Mwerinde was greatly feared by members of the cult as she was prone to violent outbursts and regularly beat members of her congregation for the slightest transgression. Could she have been the sole driving force in the cult's leadership? Were her co-leaders in fact her followers? Sadly we will never know the truth. This tragedy wiped out entire families of innocent people whose only mistake was to hope for a better life, and to trust in those who had promised them a way out of the poverty, crime and disease that surrounded them. They were led to their deaths by the twisted leaders of their church, who made promises that they could not fulfill. Rather than admit their failure and suffer the consequences, they took the lives of over eight hundred adults and children who were relying on them for a brighter future.

CHAPTER 15

The Children Of God:
Ricky Rodriguez

This final chapter is a tragic tale that is very close to my heart. Having been born and raised within this particular cult, I know from experience what pain and suffering it has imposed on its members, both adult and child. I spent the first eighteen years of my life in complete isolation from the outside world, with no knowledge of what normality was due to the brainwashing I was put through from birth.

I grew up with an acute awareness of who Ricky Rodriguez was, but he was called Davidito within the group. Often referred to as 'the prince', he was considered royal as he was the heir to the cult's throne and heralded as the one who would succeed his parents and lead the movement into the dark years that would precede the end of the world. But, in order to tell you his story, I must begin with that of his parents and the creation of this notorious sex cult.

David Brandt Berg was born in 1919 in California. The son of two dedicated Christian evangelists, he was groomed from a very young age to follow in their path and dedicate his life to religion. His Swedish father, Hjalmer Berg, very much took a backstage role and allowed his wife, Virginia Brandt, to take centre stage in their evangelical missions. As a family, they lived frugally off the donations of church members and regularly went on the road, travelling across the United States preaching in churches and leading large revivals in tabernacles such as the Miami Gospel Tabernacle, where his mother became a well-known star speaker. She was the greatest and most powerful influence in Berg's life and, as a young man, he became heavily involved in her work, often accompanying her on her trips and acting as her chauffer when required.

He married a conservative Christian girl, Jane Miller, in 1944 and they went on to have four children. He then joined the Christian and Missionary Alliance in Arizona as a minister; but, shortly after, he was told to leave when he began preaching rather controversial messages to their flock. He spent the next fifteen years travelling to various states where he held a number of pastoral and teaching jobs.

He moved to Miami, Florida, where he worked in a branch of the missionary training school, 'Soul Clinic' but, again, he was forced to move on when he went beyond the given curriculum and began preaching against the theory of evolution being taught in school. His boss transferred him to another branch in Texas where he worked for several years, but he became increasingly discontent with having to conform to the church. Therefore, when his mother invited him to join her ministry in the seaside town of Huntington Beach, California, he jumped at the opportunity.

At that time, Huntington Beach was a magnet for hippies and Berg was thrilled to have found an audience that was not only young and fresh but more importantly, were willing to reject normal society and embrace a new meaning in their lives. He began preaching in a coffee house and, before long, his radical message and charismatic personality attracted hundreds of hippies to his sermons each night. Within a couple of months he had around fifty followers who wanted to dedicate their lives to his cause. They moved in together and, in late 1968, he officially named his group 'The Children of God'.

Around this time he won over a new recruit, Karen Zerby, the daughter of a minister who was twenty-seven years younger than him. He appointed her as his secretary and began an affair with her, which ended his already troubled marriage. Once his first wife was out of the way, he made his relationship with Zerby official and proclaimed her to be his muse and queen. They married and, with her assistance, he began to issue letters to his followers. In these publications, he blasted the outside world and gave detailed instructions to his followers on how to live like a true Christian. From the practical running of their communes to personal hygiene, Berg became involved in every aspect of their lives.

In the early 1970s, the cult expanded into Europe, where they gained large numbers of new recruits who enthusiastically joined this seemingly righteous cause. Berg's teachings set his young disciples on fire. They hit the streets daily preaching about God's love and the need to reject the ways of the 'system', their term for regular society. They believed that Jesus would be returning soon and that their mission was to prepare for his coming and save as many souls as they could by bringing them to Christ and his salvation. In some cities, they went out on public vigils in large numbers wearing biblical attire and symbols. They would dress in sackcloth with ash streaked across their foreheads and an ox yolk around their neck. In one hand they would hold a long wooden staff and, in the other, a scroll with verses of doom from the Bible scrawled on it, warning people to repent or face the wrath of God.

Life in the cult was an attractive prospect for most young hippies. They lived communally in 'colonies', rejected normality, embraced free love and worked in harmony for what appeared to be a glorious cause. They spent most of their days out on the street distributing Christian literature and singing songs about God in exchange for small donations. Their evenings were spent studying the Bible, praying and dancing to inspirational tunes. As they expanded further, they attracted members from wider circles of society such as Fleetwood Mac's lead guitarist, Jeremy Spencer, and other young adults who came from wealthy families and the upper scales of society.

Berg very quickly proclaimed himself to be the Prophet of the End. Known as Moses David or 'Dad' to his followers, he believed that modern Christians had lost their way, as in his opinion, true believers were meant to live their lives as the disciples of Jesus had done in the first-century. He rejected all mainstream churches, calling them traitors of the faith, and he told his followers that, in order to live according to the way Christ intended, they had to dedicate their lives fully to the cause and separate themselves from the rest of the world. He rejected materialism and firmly believed that the end of the world was fast approaching. He preached that his calling from God was to raise an army of Christians who would fight against the Antichrist and save the lost souls of the world in the years leading up to the apocalypse.

Daily life in cult communes was strict and regulated. All members had to be focused on saving lost souls and bringing them to Jesus. No carnal or material comforts were allowed and their living arrangements ranged from campsites to squatting in empty buildings. They slept in sleeping bags and ate whatever they could afford or convince shops to donate. Members were forbidden to engage in sexual intercourse until they were married and all drugs, cigarettes, alcohol and contraception were banned.

But, after a few years of this revolutionary lifestyle, the first of many changes took place that transformed the group entirely. On a practical level, things could not remain as they were. Over the years, couples had married and were producing children at an alarming rate due to the lack of contraception and, therefore, colonies could no longer travel like vagabonds or live on the scarce minimums as they had previously done. Berg issued instructions that smaller units should unite and form larger 'homes', with detailed instructions on how the leadership structure would be formed both across the group and in each commune. He also issued a new 'move of the spirit' in which he told his followers that, due to the Western world's cold-hearted attitude towards God, they should conquer the East. This led to a large portion of cult members migrating south and east, where they concentrated heavily in Asia and South America. It was also around this time that he introduced a doctrine that would become the trademark of the cult to this day.

In what he claimed to be a revelation from God, he announced that sex was no longer restricted to married followers and he introduced 'The Law of Love'. He told his followers that there was only one law and that it was 'love'; therefore, anything done in the spirit of love was pure and acceptable. He encouraged members to 'share' sexually with other members of the group, claiming that it would teach them humility and bring them closer to one another. It began with the idea that single members should not have to be deprived of sex because of their status and, therefore, it was the duty of married members to sacrifice and share sexually with them. It was considered a demonstration of unselfishness and a way to show God's love to their brother or sister in Christ. But, before long, the doctrine expanded and all members were instructed to 'share' with each other, whether married or single. Sharing would become a significant part of members' lives for many years to come, and most of the communes took it to obsessive extremes, creating sharing schedules for members to follow, which ensured that everyone was having a turn with everyone else.

More often than not, members had no choice about who they had sex with. Such decisions were made by the leaders of the home and in some cases they were so desperate to please Berg that they instructed their residents to partake in orgies that were filmed and sent to him. This started a trend and, before long, Berg insisted on being sent a steady stream of homemade movies that captured their sexual escapades. He also instructed his female followers to perform stripteases, which he would watch while he was having sex with the women in his harem.

Once sharing was implemented, Berg dropped another bombshell on his followers. He pushed the boundaries of sexual perversion even further when he announced a new revelation he had allegedly received from God, called 'Flirty Fishing'. He had slyly begun to introduce the concept in 1976 by publishing a series of letters recounting his own experiences using Zerby, who was known as Mama Maria, as 'bait' to win a young Spanish waiter to God. He encouraged her to have sex with the young man in order to show him God's love in a tangible, physical way. The man did not join the group, but Berg told his flock that the experiment had taught him the value of showing God's love to the 'fish', his term for the those who they targeted for this new practice. He told them that God wanted them all to be willing to sacrifice their body in order to catch the fish and win them to Christ.

A handful of members left the group when this was announced, but the majority jumped on board over time. To this day, I find it incomprehensible that thousands of adults could be completely blind as to what they were being brainwashed to do. Perhaps this was due to the fact that, if a disciple doubted Berg's leadership, they would be excommunicated and sent away, forced to leave their family behind. Even if they were allowed to stay, their life would become a living nightmare with public humiliation, demotion to menial jobs and rejection by their peers. Reporting on your fellow man was an obligation: even married couples were told that they must betray their partner if they had any suspicions that they were straying from God, or beginning to doubt Berg's doctrines.

Following her encounter with the Spanish waiter, Karen Zerby fell pregnant with her first child, Ricky Rodriguez, who was given the name Davidito, after David Berg. The child was informally adopted by Berg, who proclaimed him to be his heir and the future prophet and leader of the movement who would guide the group through the last years of the earth's existence. Pretty soon, Flirty Fishing evolved, as Berg realised it could be a source of fundraising as well. It started with the theory that there was no harm in accepting gifts from the 'fish' if they wanted to show their thanks for bringing them the priceless gift that salvation was.

Before long, however, the 'gifts' became the primary reason for Flirty Fishing. Women were encouraged to place themselves in situations where they could meet wealthy men or high-ranking government officials, particularly those who could use their influence to protect the cult. It was effectively prostitution swept under a blanket of religious manipulation. The financial gain was immense and most homes relied on their regulars, who would swing by the house every so often and borrow one of the women for the night. The following morning she would return with a wad of cash, which would be handed straight over to the financial manager of the home.

Escort services were introduced soon after as a more efficient form of Flirty Fishing. In a letter, Berg explained that some of the women, whom he called 'hookers for Jesus', were so concerned about making their financial targets that they were losing sight of their primary goal, which was to bring the men to salvation. He told them that, by becoming escorts, they would have an easier time meeting men and would be guaranteed payment at the end of the night. This would allow them to focus solely on talking to them about God, although they were still expected to engage in sexual intercourse with them if they so desired.

As this sexual revolution exploded, Berg was busy restructuring his leadership team and, in 1978, he renamed the group 'The Family of Love' (later known as 'The Family International'). He excommunicated those in his leadership team who had become too powerful, and put in place a lower level structure that allowed him to maintain full control of the daily running of the cult. Each home had a team of 'shepherds' who took care of the daily running of the home, from administration to allocating tasks and managing its finances.

Berg and his entire leadership team went into hiding. The location of the cult's headquarters became a highly guarded secret that was only disclosed to a handful of Berg's closest assistants. All photographs of them were destroyed to protect their identity and it remained that way until Berg's death many years later. The leaders lied to their followers, claiming that they had to go underground because government officials worldwide were trying to stop God's work. But the truth was that Interpol was looking for them. Their Flirty Fishing antics had attracted police attention and Berg was wanted on pimping and fraud charges. Tax evasion and travelling under fake identities were also added to the list of charges that he faced and he went on the run to avoid trouble. He was never caught, but he spent the rest of his life looking over his shoulder.

By 1982, the cult had around 10,000 members living in over 1,500 homes worldwide. As there were increasing numbers of children, Rodriguez's nanny, Sara Kelley, published a book that followed his upbringing, and that of her own daughter Davida. By this time, Berg's view of the 'Law of Love' had extended to the second generation. He wrote that children in the cult should be encouraged to explore their sexuality from birth and should be raised to think of sex as a natural act rather than something to be ashamed of. Horrifically, although many cult members took these letters to be a theory and not something to be practised, it was soon made apparent that, in Berg's house, they practised what he preached.

The book that Kelley and the leadership published was entitled *The Story of Davidito*. In it, she chronicled each stage of Rodriguez's childhood, including the sexual experiments that they subjected him to from a very young age. The book had photographs of Rodriguez as a toddler, lying with naked women, touching their breasts and being fondled. One image in particular depicted Kelley giving Rodriguez fellatio at the age of three, with a caption explaining that Berg had suggested that she do so to loosen the foreskin on his penis. She also explained that Berg fondly remembered instances when his own nanny would suck him to sleep during his naptime at the age of six. The photos were accompanied by detailed accounts of the 'love up sessions' the many women in the home had with Rodriguez, as well as the sessions that they arranged between him and his playmate Davida, in which they encouraged the children to touch each other. On a few occasions, Kelley describes how the children would wander around the communal room and watch the adults as they engaged in an orgy. And in one chapter, Kelley describes how seventeen-month-old Rodriguez watched a couple having sex in the pool and jokes that he was trying to imitate their movement by wiggling his bottom and moving his hand up and down.

Some scenes describe 'love up sessions' with Kelley or his second nanny, Angela Smith, in such sickening detail that it leaves absolutely no doubt that

Rodriguez was sexually abused on a daily basis over many years. Throughout the book, Kelley expresses her opinion that the toddlers loved their sexual experiences and kept on asking for more. It is as if she is trying to justify her actions, or somehow make such a disgusting crime appear innocent and beneficial to them. Kelley also insists on several occasions that these practices should be kept within the group, as outsiders would not understand the spirit of love and freedom which inspired it. To me, this shows that she was fully aware that what she was doing was wrong and perverse, and yet she carried on for a number of years.

This book would be the catalyst that started a wave of child abuse. Sexual freedom and the Law of Love remained very much an active practice for many years and we children were caught in the middle, exposed to sex from the time we could open our eyes. As a young child, I recall walking past rooms and seeing couples having sex on the bed. I hardly flinched over it as I had been taught that there was nothing wrong with sex and nudity; and yet, my stomach would churn when I would see it. Rodriguez's childhood was no different; in fact, it was most likely the worst. Due to the fact he lived his life in the seclusion and secrecy of the royal household, little was known until much later.

Eventually, after allegations of abuse hit the media in 1986, the cult was forced to ban all sexual activities with minors. However, I can assure you, from my own experience, that not only sexual abuse but physical, emotional and psychological abuse, remained rampant throughout the cult for a number of years following the ban. Members lived under a mountain of rules that dominated their daily lives. Privacy was non-existent, even the thoughts in your head. Children were separated from their parents and lived in groups with other children of a similar age. Our daily routine was gruelling, with hours of religious studies that included pages of Berg's quotes that had to be memorised; chores around the house would take place for a few hours each day, and no one was allowed to leave the compound unless they had been given permission to do so by the home shepherds.

Paranoia across the group increased as the years went by. Berg believed that Antichrist soldiers were after us and, hence, we had to live in secrecy, as if we were criminals on the run. We children could easily go for a year or more without leaving the property, often only being let out to accompany our parents on trips to the border to renew our visas. No outside influences were allowed. Only a handful of 'system' movies were permitted, such as *The Sound of Music*, Shirley Temple's *Heidi* and biblical dramas. Cult-produced videos, music and books were provided in order to limit any outside influences and we were made to fear 'pollution' from the 'system'.

Berg predicted the end of the world several times, but each time it fell through and the entire cult was made to fast and pray for days on end. Berg would accuse his followers of causing the delays, telling them that it was not taking place because they were spiritually unprepared for it.

As the years went by, they cleaned up their outside image in order to escape suspicion and legal issues. After Berg's death in 1994, a child custody case took place in the UK which exposed the child abuse allegations. The cult's new leaders, Zerby and her lover, Peter Kelly, conveniently blamed Berg for all the abuse that had occurred, claiming that he should have made it clearer that his doctrines were spiritual and not necessarily meant to be practised. In order to win the case, they were forced to make this declaration to the judge, but did so in secret and cult members only found out about it years later. They truly did shoot themselves in the foot as, despite having ordered members to destroy all copies of *The Story of Davidito*, ex-members had retained copies and later uploaded portions onto the internet, proving their admission to be completely false and deceptive.

At this stage, Zerby was still hopeful that her son would one day replace her as leader of the cult and she kept a very close eye on him, monitoring his every move and allowing him little interaction with people outside her headquarters, and no access at all to the outside world.

As the second generation grew into young adults, many left the cult, escaping a lifetime of oppression to brave the alien world that normal society was to us. I escaped as soon as I turned eighteen and began my own difficult journey to adapt in a world that I knew nothing about. In my bid to overcome past trauma and build a new life, I tried my best to avoid anything that was linked to the cult; however, in 2005, I was shocked when a gruesome event hit the news.

Ricky Rodriguez had committed suicide after brutally murdering his former nanny, Angela Smith. Suddenly, a flood of memories came rushing back and I was devastated that the cult had claimed yet another victim. I remember staring at the news report in complete disbelief. It was very brief and it was not until months later that the missing pieces of the puzzle came together to portray the tragic life and untimely death of the boy who was meant to be the king.

The future that Berg bestowed on Rodriguez was not only to become the next leader. He had prophesied that he and his mother, Zerby, were destined to fulfil the roles of the two last witnesses from the Book of Revelation in the Bible. They would lead not only the cult, but also all other Christians, into the final battle against the Antichrist. He prophesied that they would both die as martyrs for the cause and would receive elevated status in heaven because of their sacrifice. This prediction must have had a terrible effect on Ricky at such a young age. He had to grow up with the thought that he would inevitably die a horrible death because it was his mission.

Berg also told his followers that Davida was going to be Rodriguez's future Queen and he carried out a mock wedding to join them in marriage. After

Rodriguez's death, the dam of secrets broke and Davida went public with details of her childhood, claiming that both she and Rodriguez had been forced into sexual intercourse from an early age, not only with each other but with Berg and Zerby as well. The depraved leader would call them into his room and let them watch cartoons and eat sweets before 'love up time'. For Davida, up until the age of twelve, 'love up time' consisted of masturbation and oral sex with Berg, while Rodriguez had sexual intercourse with one of his nannies next to them. After the age of twelve, the expectations changed as they were considered adults; full intercourse became a part of the sordid sessions that were imposed on them.

There were also widely spread rumours that Rodriguez was made to have regular sex with his own mother, but Zerby denies this adamantly and, through her spokesperson, pointed out that Ricky never made that allegation himself. But, in truth, I wonder what man would admit to having had sex with his mother? Judging from his upbringing and the brainwashing he had been subjected to since birth, it is possible that he was conditioned to physically enjoy it and, once he realised the truth as an adult, could never bring himself to admit that it had happened. The very thought of his own young body being physically aroused by his mother would have been so repulsive he would have felt sick and damaged beyond repair.

Such stories are even more believable when one considers that others had accused Berg of incest in the past. His eldest daughter, Deborah, published a book in which she claimed that her father had tried to have sex with her on several occasions. In a transcript of a meeting that he held with his senior management team, Berg brags of his capacity to multitask and tells his audience that, while he was speaking, he was 'goosing' his youngest daughter, Faithy, under the table with his toes. I saw this document with my own eyes when I was a young child and I recall feeling sick when I read it. No matter how much brainwashing I had been through, my mind refused to consider it acceptable.

Following Berg's death and his mother's marriage to Kelly, Rodriguez struggled to maintain the image that his foster father had imposed on him. He had been raised as royalty and trained since birth to take over the group's leadership. His mother, Zerby, was thriving as leader; she had wowed her followers by introducing the 'Loving Jesus' doctrine, in which she told members they should take their relationship with Jesus to a new level by including him in their sex lives. Graphic suggestions were given of crude sex talk that could be used to show Jesus how much we desired him; I was a teenager when these letters were published and I recall feeling quite embarrassed when I read them. To prove that they were embracing the concept at cult headquarters, Zerby referred to their home as, 'The House of the Open Pussy'. I assume she felt that this was a fun and revolutionary way of demonstrating how open and willing they were to God's new incentives, which always seemed to be linked to sex.

Zerby had been going blind for years, but her lack of vision only caused her to keep a tighter rein on Rodriguez to ensure that he would not stray from the future that she and Berg had planned for him. But, at the age of eighteen, he became restless, and so she sent him to live in a selection of carefully chosen communes, the plan being that his belief in the cause would be rekindled by mingling with other young people in the group. However, she also hoped that his presence in ordinary homes would reinforce the leadership's decreasing popularity among second generation memberes across the group.

At the age of nineteen, and during one of his stays in a regular community home in Eastern Europe, he met Alexia, a dark-haired teenager who he was instantly attracted to. Before long, they became a couple. However, their intense romance was hindered by the fact that sharing sexually with others was still rampantly practised and, as the future leader of the group, Rodriguez had to show his support of the doctrine by not only sharing himself sexually with the other women in the home, but also by sharing his newfound love with other men. Before long, he began to rebel against the future that his mother and Berg had imposed on him and he decided that he could not live with it any more.

They left the cult together in 2000 and moved to Tacoma in the Pacific Northwest of the United States, as they knew a handful of ex-members who lived there. Rodriguez got a job as a shipping clerk and he and Alexia married, moving into a cheap apartment with only the bare essentials. But they didn't care. They needed nothing more than each other and the freedom to make their own choices in life.

Unfortunately, even that period of calm was not enough to quench the growing unease in Rodriguez's mind. Several ex-members contacted him and told him of the abuse that they had suffered and the psychological trauma that they continued to endure as a result. They began pressuring him to take a stand against the cult, as his upbringing in the leadership household meant that he was privy to information and experiences that could bring justice to all those that had suffered in silence. Having been raised to be a leader, he could not shake the guilt that he felt towards these young ex-members and he began to believe that it was his calling in life to carry out justice for his peers. He felt somehow that he owed it to them. In his opinion, he had no right to move on and attempt to have a happy life when other ex-members were suffering and unable to get over their pain.

Before long, his self-inflicted guilt overwhelmed him and he began to think of revenge. In the summer of 2004, he left Alexia and headed to Arizona with one thought in mind. He was on a quest to find his mother. The one question that will never be answered is the following. Was his mission simply to confront his mother in order to get answers to the many questions he had about his past? Or was it always his plan to kill her and, by doing so, gain some sort of revenge? Zerby's whereabouts had been a secret for years and Rodriguez was no exception. Now that he had left the cult, he was considered a possible traitor and someone who could not be trusted.

It was in January 2005, just days before his thirtieth birthday, that Rodriguez recorded an hour long home video that would shock the world and throw the group into the spotlight again. In the video clip, heavy metal music booms in the background as Rodriguez faces the camera. His face is sweaty and flustered and his eyes are heavy with exhaustion and the darkness of hate.

Anyway, well Mom's gonna pay for that. She's gonna pay dearly, one way or another. If I don't get to her, man, if I don't get to her, and life goes on, I'm gonna keep hunting her in the next life, let me tell you. And I wanna keep going until somebody gets her, I get her, justice will be done. Believe me, it's only a matter of time. Somehow, someway, it's gonna happen. I'm gonna try to do my part. We'll see what happens. We'll go from there.

A few months earlier, Rodriguez had moved to Tucson, Arizona, as he heard that his mother had recently visited his grandparents, who lived in a retirement home near the city. Following that discovery, he decided to lie in wait for her there, convinced that she would return one day. Judging by the video, it seems that, at this point, he had already decided to end his own life, but his plan was to get to his mother first.

Anyway, okay, I'm sorry I'm getting all off track here. Where the fuck was I? Suicide. Yes suicide. Horrible. A horrible thing when adults contemplate suicide, but it's so much worse when you got a fuckin' little kid who is, you know, not born to be a messed up little fucker. But he's a little life, ya know, she's a little life, and you just fuck 'em over because you're a sick fuckin' pervert, and you don't have anything better to do with your life than to fuck up your little kids. It's just so far beyond me, I just can't fuckin' imagine it. But yet it happened. It happened right before me. It happened to all of you. Thousands of us, some worse than others.

I had it good in many ways. I didn't get fucked in the ass, you know, I was a guy. A lot of you girls, phew, crap, I can't even compare my stories with yours... There's so many other kinds of abuse that went on, that to some of us were just as bad, and some of us didn't have it that bad. So I'm not gonna sit here and say, 'oh yeah, I had it the worst or I didn't,' because it really doesn't matter. It should never have happened at all. To anybody. That's the point. So that's when I started contemplating suicide. And I've been fuckin' thinkin' about it ever since.

Ah, I've tried so many things, trying to, trying to somehow fit in. Somehow to find, you know, a normal life. Everybody has said who I talked to about this, well you know, that everybody has their problems in this fucked-up life. But those people who say that, you know, they don't have a clue as to what actually went on. I mean, 'cos, they weren't part of the cult.

Anyway, ah, so I always figured that, and I always still think about suicide, and I try to push it away. I'm successful for a while, but it'd always come back. Started coming back more frequently, those thoughts, and uh, and I just, I just wanted it to end. That was my hope.

But you know what I feel that that would be the selfish thing to do. That would be the, the quitter's way out, because yeah, I'm sorta quitting right now, but in a way I'm not, because I'm not doing it the way I wanna do it. I'm trying to do something lasting. Something that, God forbid in the next life, if it does go on, I can look back at this if I'm able to and, and know that okay maybe I didn't technically do the right thing but I tried to do something to help. I didn't just fade away, I didn't just turn tail and run and let those fuckers win, but I did what I could to make a difference. And I don't know how really far I'm gonna get, but I'm starting to think now that it's not gonna be that far... well I'll get one person, that's for sure. My source for information. Uh, the goal is to bring down those sick fuckers – Mama (Karen Zerby) and Peter (Peter Kelly). My own mother! What an evil little cunt. Goddamn! How can you do that to kids? How can you do that to kids and sleep at night? I don't fuckin' know. Anyway, that's my goal. But, I'm one person. I'm working under, eh, situations that aren't that great right now because I'll only have a small window of opportunity to, ah, get the information that I need out of this person.'

As I listened to him say those words, I could hear the profound hatred in his voice. If his mother had not directly abused him, would he have such bitterness against her?

He got into contact with his aunt who lived nearby and who he knew had a negative opinion of his mother and the cult. His aunt and uncle tried the best they could to support Rodriguez in what they thought was an attempt at a fresh start, but they had no idea what he was really there for. He found a job as an electrician and joined a local gun club. Then, he waited for his mother to return while he continuously sent messages to her assistants, hoping to lure her into meeting him.

As with so many events that occurred in our past, we will never know the full truth of what brought this explosive situation to such a disastrous end. Many say that Zerby sent Angela Smith as a scout, to assess whether the situation was safe for her to eventually meet him herself. Zerby disputes this and states that Smith had recently left the cult and went to meet Rodriguez of her own accord. Friends of Rodriguez claim that he had arranged to meet Smith with the intention of extracting information from her as to his mother's whereabouts. Rodriguez seems to validate this in his video when he refers to his, 'source of information'; but little did his friends know what lengths he was prepared to go to in order to get that information.

At one point in the video, he begins to display various objects and weapons in front of the camera as he explains what they are for.

I went with a Glock 23, forty-calibre. I thought of nine millimetre—I think everybody does—the reason is, that I didn't go with a nine, is that there is the great debate always, because the nine-millimetre people say that their guns are the greatest thing since sliced fuckin' bread. Um, the ammo's cheap. They're effective.

But, but I'll tell you if these go through somebody's skull, this fucker's gonna expand, so that's what I'm counting on...but the truth is this is my weapon of choice... The k-bar knife. Served marines for many, many years...I only want it for one purpose, and that is taking out the scum, taking out the fuckin' trash... So one shot, one kill. Well, hopefully. Anyway, we'll see about that. Then I have some smaller knives and stuff... So anyway, duct tape. You can fix anything with this fuckin' stuff. Yeah, I'm gonna fix some people with this.

I'm not trained in torture methods, which is why I'm gonna have to make do. I got my drill here. The reason why it's got this fuckin' padding here is just to try and silence it a bit, 'cos I'm going to be in an apartment. Um, I got gags, fuckin' socks, and lots of fuckin' duct tape. Um, I got a soldering iron. Heat. I've got a crude implement I think can work wonders, especially if it is used in the right way. But I'm not trained. I don't know how to fuckin' do this. I don't wanna fuckin' do this! Goddamn it! Oh, you gotta see this. This is not for torture, but man, it could be. The stun-master. 775,000 volts! You gotta hear this puppy. Wow! That's got to scare anybody. But it's not going to be used for scaring. It's gonna be used for temporarily incapacitating them. It is a non-lethal weapon.

It was early in the morning on 9 January 2005 that they found Rodriguez dead in his car.

The previous night he had 'phoned his wife Alexia and spoken to her for hours as he drove through the desert, fleeing from the crime that he had just committed. He told her that he had taken revenge and that there was a body in his flat. He kept telling her over and over again that he was exhausted, having not slept in two days; and towards the end of the call he expressed his desire to end it all.

At some point after his 'phone call to Alexia, he stopped for a rest in Blythe, California, where he checked into a Holiday Inn Express. There he showered, drank beer and watched television. He then drove a short distance to a quiet road, where he shot himself in the head. The weapon he used was the very same Glock handgun that he had displayed in his video. By this time, his wife had called Tucson police and told them about her 'phone call with Rodriguez. There, in the blood-splattered apartment, they found the body of Angela Smith. She lay dead on the carpet in a foetal position with her hands joined, as if in prayer. Her throat had been slashed and she had defensive wounds to her arms. Despite the threats that he made in his recording, he had not tortured her. In his final 'phone call to Alexia, he described her final moments in these chilling words.

> The hardest thing about it was that as she lay dying, she still didn't understand what she had done.

He had already expressed his deep frustration in his recording, when he talked about his childhood friend, Davida.

> I got in contact with my sister. Well, I consider her my sister because to me she is. She's not flesh and blood, but uh, I'm talking about uh Davida... She's, yeah, she's a, um, dancing in New York.
>
> Um, anyway she calls me sometimes and we talk. She tells me the stuff she's going through, and she's, breaks my heart, you know, 'cos I want to help her. But there's nothing I can do because it's all up here (points to his head), you know, the damage has been done. I'm not saying she's crazy, but she has nightmares at night. I guess a lot of us do. I have nightmares, but not really about the same things, but about the cult. Um, she has nightmares about, uh, being dragged out of bed in the middle of the night to go have sex with, uh, Berg...Where's our apology? They're not even fuckin' sorry. They're not even fucking sorry. Can you imagine?
>
> But I don't know—it's harder than I thought it would be. But, yeah, I don't really have anything to lose, I think, and ah, yeah, I don't want to go through my life, um, the way it is now. I've tried for four years... And uh, everyday, if it had just gotten a little better, a little better. Even emotionally, mentally, for me, and it would have been okay. It would have given me hope. But it's gotten worse. Every fucking day has been a little worse than the day before.

Rodriguez's death brought the number of ex-member suicides to approximately forty, though the true number will never be known as most second generation members dispersed and disappeared into society after they escaped the cult.

What went through Rodriguez's mind in the last forty-eight hours of his life will always be a mystery. Perhaps he felt that killing someone was his only way of getting the outside world's attention, as it would have been impossible for him to prove anything in a court of law. I know the feeling only too well as, by the time we were old enough to take action against the cult, they had cleaned up their act and erased that part of their past. It was as if our suffering had never existed. These were Rodriguez's final words on the video clip:

> You know anger does not begin—does not begin—to describe how I feel about these people and what they've done. You know, I mean, rage! Uh, I get livid, you know? Just, that's a little closer to the way I feel. And uh, that's gonna feel good to do some damage even if it's not much. As far as I can go. That's what I'm gonna do. It's gonna feel so fucking good—liberating. So, anyway, what can I say? I guess I said it all.
>
> Alright. Oh well—keep fighting. Keep the faith, and all that other stuff, and someday—in some way—some of us are gonna be around to see those fuckers burn. Literally or figuratively—they're going down. So with that happy thought, I shall leave you.

Did Angela Smith deserve such a death? In my opinion, no one deserves such a thing. A defenceless woman of fifty-one years of age should not have been murdered in such a way, whether she committed those acts of child abuse in a state of brainwash or knowingly. She should, however, have been brought before a court of law and punished accordingly. But I can understand how Ricky never saw that as an option, as none of us had enough evidence to build a case. Even though so many accusations have been made by ex-members, often against the same individuals, we second generation ex-members know that we could never win in a court of law. Most of the witnesses would refuse to come forward or deny having witnessed any of it, out of fear that they would be considered accomplices of the crime.

Rodriguez's story is yet another very sad tale of the disastrous consequences that a cult experience can have on a person; particularly on a child who is born into such a sordid world and is brainwashed from their very first breath.

Epilogue

Cults can hide in many places. They are so adept at blending into society and masking their true colours that often their victims do not realise that they were even in a cult until they have escaped it. Nor do they fully comprehend the severity of the brainwashing that they were subjected to, until they are finally free of it.

I am often asked how a group of people can come to accept such bizarre and, at times, perverse doctrines. To answer that, one must understand the concept of 'groupthink' and the process of brainwashing.

The initial research on groupthink was conducted by Irvine Janis, a research psychologist from Yale University, who carried out a series of experiments that brought astounding results. One of his many experiments involved placing a group of people in a room, to run through a series of logic cards. Each one required a simple response that would be considered obvious to anyone who had even a limited education. Everyone in the room, apart from the person being tested, was briefed in advance and told to give the incorrect response to certain cards.

In the first round of questions, the person being tested responded correctly, despite the incorrect answers that were given by the other people in the room. But, as the next rounds took place, he began to hesitate and, ultimately, after several rounds, he responded incorrectly, despite having passed those very same questions in previous rounds. He was swayed by the group around him and conformed to the responses that they gave. Such an experiment is very powerful and demonstrates the same pattern that occurs in a cult environment. With the addition of brainwashing, complete control can be achieved over a group of people who become unable to differentiate the cult's 'truth' from reality.

Often called 'thought reform', brainwashing takes place in two stages. First it begins with the breakdown of the victim's personality and integrity.

Everything they once knew to be the truth is called into question, including their view of what is right and wrong. They are made to question their own way of thinking, leading them to become completely submissive and receptive to the cult. Once that phase is complete, the victim is like a blank canvas, ripe for reprogramming. In the second stage, cult doctrines and beliefs are fed to the victim relentlessly until they can no longer think or act without the cult's direction. This transformed individual is often completely unrecognisable to their family and friends; it is as if they have had a personality transplant. Such a result cannot be achieved in a matter of days. Brainwashing in a cult takes place over a number of years.

New recruits are drawn into what appears to be a mystical world, or an environment that is extremely warm and friendly. From the start, they are made to feel immense gratitude for being permitted to take part in the mission that the cult has adopted. When you analyse the history of most religious cults, they generally start out preaching very acceptable doctrines during their early years, which is the period in which they recruit the majority of their disciples. But, like a flesh-eating plant, once their prey is drawn in, the trap closes around them. New recruits would not even know that this is taking place, as they would be so engrossed in their new life that they would be oblivious to small changes happening around them. Even if something raises an obvious red flag, the person in question cannot see it; that is until they escape the cult and then realise that they were blinded to it. Then, over a period of months and years, the cult's doctrines become more bizarre and radical, but often in such a gradual manner that followers do not find it a great leap to move from one to the next.

We can clearly see this pattern occur in the Children of God. It started with one wonderful word—love. In the cult's early days, they were very conservative when it came to sex and their notion of love was platonic, with cult members constantly 'love bombing' (hugging each other) and sharing their love for God through singing and dancing.

Not long after, it became slightly less conservative and they allowed married couples to take on a third partner and form threesomes. Following that, 'sharing' was introduced, which began as a seemingly innocent concept but which, over a couple of years, turned the cult into a sex-mad fellowship, obsessed with orgies and promiscuity. Then came 'flirty fishing' which, to the outside world, was prostitution pure and simple. But by this stage, cult members were so desensitised to sex that they hardly flinched. Those who did were condemned and made to feel as if there was something wrong with them, but the majority had been stripped of all their inhibitions and moved on to that next step with ease. Not long after that, Berg shared his opinion that children should also be uninhibited sexually, a doctrine that every closet paedophile in the cult took as their green card to abuse children around them.

If we take a step back and compare both ends of the spectrum, we can see how they went from being a highly conservative movement to a sex obsessed cult who practiced prostitution as if it was a sacred mission from God, and whose leaders encouraged child sex as a pure and natural act. All this took place over just a few years. Cults are very difficult for authorities to pin down, mainly due to the world of secrecy that they live in. Often they hide behind religious freedom and cry religious persecution if authorities begin to take an interest in them. It is very difficult to find witnesses that are prepared to speak out and, if they do, those witnesses are often so blinded to the truth that not much useful information can be gleaned from them. This makes it very difficult for any criminal prosecutions to take place, and so often, cults can operate undetected for many years.

Cults come in many shapes and forms as each has their own specific doctrines and methods of manipulation. But, more often than not, they share general characteristics which can be used to identify them from other religious groups. Here are some of the tell-tale signs to look out for:

Control Through Fear of Punishment

This is often achieved through psychological coercion, due to members living with the threat of physical or spiritual punishment hanging over them at all times. They are usually retained in the cult through threats of separation from their family, warnings of an afterlife in hell or some other form of divine punishment. Confessions are encouraged or required and self-criticism is enforced. Members who voice doubt or question the cult are often humiliated in front of their peers; their ego and any shred of self-dignity and pride is broken down, which leads the person in question to lose their confidence and will power.

Isolation from Outside Influences

Cult members are usually limited or banned from accessing outside media or literature, to avoid influences that are not in line with cult doctrines and practices. This can include being kept in the dark as to current events taking place in the world outside, or being given a cult version of those events. Communication with outsiders is limited, if not banned, in order to maintain utter control.

Physical and Psychological Exhaustion

Often, cult members are overworked or subjected to gruelling schedules, so that they are too exhausted to analyse the situation around them or put up a fight against their leaders. They are often mentally worn down by long barrages of doctrines being fed to them on a daily basis, the end result being a person who is too weak to think rationally, let alone question what they are being made to believe.

Totalitarian Society

Cult leaders demand total, unwavering loyalty. Members often idolise or worship their leader and believe that he or she can do no wrong. They are often convinced that everything their leader says or does is flawless; the instinct to question, doubt or challenge what they are being told is weak or absent altogether. Occasionally, this will extend to the leader claiming to be God or a prophet; hence, all salvation and access to a higher spiritual level must go through them.

Fear of 'Enemies'

The enemy in question is usually the outside world or a specific government or legal body. By instilling fear in their followers, cults are able to keep them deeply dependant on the organisation for safety and protection. Creating such an 'enemy' is also used to enhance unity and prove to their followers that their mission must be so extraordinary if outsiders are trying to shut them down.

A False Front

Cults will regularly operate under a front such as a non-profit organisation, a humanitarian association, self-help or life coaching groups, exclusive clubs, New Age spiritualist groups or fanatic 'prepper' communities. There is no limit to where they can hide. As we know from our chapter on Shoko Asahara's Aum Shinrikyo, what may appear to be an innocent yoga retreat could turn out to be more than you bargained for. And, as with Luc Jouret of the Order of the Solar Temple, seminars on alternative medicines and esoteric healing were his hunting ground for new recruits.

The Breakdown of Family Units and Relationships

Cults very often use the threat of separation to maintain control over their followers, who fear being sent away from their spouse or children. True friendships and relationships are often impossible as cult members are encouraged or forced to betray their friends and family members, as they have been brainwashed to believe that their loyalty to them comes second to their loyalty towards the cult. Even close family units are damaged as a result and there is an intense feeling of isolation and loneliness for members, who are unable to trust or confide in those closest to them.

Extreme Loyalty

Cult members are prepared to do anything that the cult asks of them. They are often willing to go to any length to defend, protect or maintain the image of the cult. For example, telling lies to authorities. In the Children of God, they created a term for this called 'heavenly deception', which was their belief that it was acceptable to be dishonest, deceptive or even to commit a crime, if it was necessary to protect the cult and 'God's work'. On a more serious level, this can be taken to extreme lengths such as committing murder or suicide to protect the cult or simply, because their leader has told them to do so.

Financial Control and Exploitation

In most cases, cult members are not allowed to manage their own income which makes it very difficult for them to be independent or to escape, should they wish to. Cult money regularly disappears up the leadership ranks and members do not see the benefits. Often, followers are not only exploited financially, but physically through labour, or being given no choice as to what role they play in the cult's daily activities. In many cases, they are made to earn money but are not allowed to keep any of it for their personal use.

Sexual Abuse

Very often, cult leaders and their leadership team will exploit cult members sexually, using their position to gain sexual favours from their followers and at times, their children. They often use sex as a tool to exert their power over their followers, as was the case with Charles Manson. For example, if a cult member is becoming too outspoken, a leader may demand sex with his or her spouse to remind them of their place in the hierarchy. This can be taken to the extreme, with more powerful members of the cult forcing their often perverse fantasies on their followers.

Cults cause even more damage to children who are born and raised within their environment. Brainwashing is no longer a two-stage process as innocent babies are born a blank canvas, and therefore phase two can commence immediately from birth. These children are raised with no notion of what a normal environment is and in most cases, are kept completely out of contact with the outside world. From my own personal experience, I can confirm that it is a very psychologically damaging environment to grow up in. There is a famous saying, 'you can't miss what you don't know,' but most cult-raised individuals would disagree with that. From a young age I knew that something was not right about the environment around me but I had no way of knowing what it was. I permanently felt unsafe and uncared for, but was violently punished for my withdrawn demeanour.

Only as an adolescent did I become aware that my family's lifestyle was not only unusual, but downright bizarre. Like criminals on the run, we moved from city to city across South East Asia, with no permanent home and with the threat of attack hanging over us at all times. After all, we believed that the outside world was out to destroy us and that the Antichrist's army would impose martyrdom on us at any moment. It was a life of permanent paranoia and anxiety, but the real hardship began when I finally escaped the cult.

It is very difficult to describe how it was, but I often ask people to try to imagine that they were dropped off on an alien planet that is completely different to anything that they have previously known. I did not have the first clue what a bank account was, or how to apply for a job. Unfortunately, search engines were not around in those days and it took me weeks to figure out what a Curriculum Vitae was or how to dress for a job interview. I was lucky enough to speak English but when I arrived in London, I realised that the English I spoke was a cult version, with terms that did not even exist in the regular English language. For the first few years I felt completely isolated, as if I did not belong in the world. Many of my peers who had also left the cult were driven to substance abuse and even suicide as they were unable to make the transition. Despite a few close calls, I consider myself lucky to have escaped, and to have been able to integrate the world and build a normal life.

Those who join a cult as an adult are not necessarily better off. The longer they are 'inside', the longer it takes for the effects of brainwashing to wear off. I have spoken with ex-members who, even having left the Children of God several years ago, are still in denial and defend certain practices. One moment they are filled with resentment and hatred for the movement that destroyed their life and the next, they are giving feeble excuses, perhaps in an attempt to soothe the guilt that they feel. Unless they were directly involved in a crime, I do not blame them, but rather hope that one day they will be mentally free from the cult's clutches, and will be able to find peace.

Religion and spirituality can, and should be, a wonderful asset in a person's life. But too often, when it becomes organised, it turns into a source of evil that inflicts pain on those involved. There are far too many perverse individuals who are prepared to take advantage of those who have a faith and who are looking to create a better world. Extremists and cults are the poison of religions that could be a benefit to society; they take advantage of those who dream to make a difference, and they use them to cause destruction in the name of their 'God'.

Religion should be used to spread compassion, love and humanity, and many great personalities have done so throughout history. For example, Mother Teresa, who lived her life driven by her faith, which translated into compassion and love for her fellow man. But sadly, a few extremists and power-hungry individuals have ruined the reputation of all those who seek to do good. They have used religion as a vehicle for terror and destruction, with no regard as to who they have destroyed on their mission for power and fame.

The best way to avoid being drawn into a cult is to thoroughly investigate spiritual or religious groups before you decide to join them. Stay far away from organisations that you are unsure of and seek help if you feel that you have fallen into a trap.

Despite the stigma, people who are deceived by cults are not naïve. Many are intelligent, successful members of society who have loving, supportive families. But, once a cult has tightened its grip on a person, it changes them dramatically and they become a ghost of who they once were. Their personality is stripped and they are no longer able to make informed decisions or think rationally. Instead, they become part of a wider group, on whom they rely on for instructions on how they should feel and what decisions they should make.

There is truly nothing more heart-breaking than to witness the state of a loved one who is under the influence of a cult. There is a feeling of helplessness, when you realise that there is very little you can do to help someone who is fully loyal to their cult, and considers you, and the rest of the world as their enemy. The best that you can do is to hope that, with time, they will come around.

Incredibly, and despite my own experiences, I still have my own faith; but my beliefs are now a blend of spiritual concepts and I keep my spiritual life private, as I do not think it is right for any person to impose their beliefs on another. In my opinion, religions should not be automatically accepted as a whole, but analysed and purged of anything that could have a negative or unhealthy impact. I do not differentiate people of different faiths as I believe that all religions can be both good and evil, depending on what the believer takes from their faith and how they apply it throughout their life. The extended research I have done on various religions has, unfortunately, led me to conclude that organised religion so often leads to disaster and death, no matter how many precautions are taken.

Cults will always exist. But we have to keep hope that raising awareness of the damage that they cause, will limit the number of souls that will be claimed by them. Once inside, there is so often, no way out but I have hope that our society is now increasingly aware of the danger that they represent, and that the generations to come, will tread into their faiths with caution.

No truer words were spoken on the subject than those of political thinker, Charles de Secondat.

> Religious wars are not caused by the fact that there is more than one religion, but by the spirit of intolerance ... the spread of which can only be regarded as the total eclipse of human reason.